Swing Trading for Beginners

The Complete Guide on How to Become a Profitable Trader Using These Proven Swing Trading Techniques and Strategies. Includes Stocks, Options, ETFs, Forex, & Futures

Adam Edwards

Table of Contents

Introduction

First, I want to thank you for choosing this book to help you learn about swing trading. The goal of this book is to help you along your journey to becoming a successful swing trader. As I will discuss later, it is important to make sure that you do your research before and after you start your career as a swing trader. I am honored that you selected this book to help you learn about swing trading. As you will be able to see from the bibliography, I have selected dozens of educational resources for the research of this book. It is my hope that my book helps ease your research by giving you the information you need to begin your journey.

In the first chapter, I will give you an introduction to financial trading. This chapter will not only describe the difference between investing and trading but it will also give you three key concepts of financial trading, such as asking yourself what you are trading and who is completing the trade. I will then explain the different types of brokers and what rights you have when you find a broker who you want to work with. I will then end this chapter by discussing the two stock market conditions that you will get to know as a swing trader.

In chapter two, I will give you a thorough introduction to what swing trading is and what it isn't. I will briefly discuss why you will want to pick swing trading over day trading. I want to focus on this because people are often confused between swing trading and day trading. I will then discuss the different stock trends, how you can decide what the right stocks are for you, and then give you a few ideas on what type of stock you can look out for as a swing trader.

In chapter three, I will look at the various financial instruments that are a part of the investing world. For example, I will take a look at options, ETFs, futures, and stocks.

Chapter four will look at how you need to treat swing trading like a professional business and not a hobby, which is often a mistake for beginners. In this chapter, I will help you walk through the process of how you will start to build your swing trading career. First, I will discuss how you can establish your own business plan, which is often referred to as a trading plan. I will then discuss how you have to make sure to set your daily schedule and how important this is to stick to. Of course, I will end out the chapter by discussing how you want to take your new career seriously, but not too serious because you don't want to become burnt-out due to working too hard as a swing trader.

In chapter five, you will learn the art of swing trading. In this chapter, I will discuss the beginning steps that you will take; such as research, finding a broker, simulation trading, and making swing trading your new career. For the second half of this chapter, I will discuss what a swing trader's day looks like. You will learn how your typical day will go from the time you start your work day to the time you close when the stock market closes, and how you need to perform your post-trading analysis.

Chapter six takes a look at the various trading strategies that you will run into as a swing trader. I first begin this chapter by discussing trend following, which is not only a strategy but one of the most important factors when it comes to analyzing your reports. You will then learn about short interest, news playing, breakouts and breakdowns, and a couple of others.

In chapter seven, I will look at the art of

selling short. While this is a strategy that you will use when the stock market is facing poor conditions, I have given this strategy its own chapter because it is often confusing to many beginners. Therefore, I wanted to spend more time explaining short selling in a way that you are most likely to understand. Of course, I will not only discuss the process of short selling, but I will also look at the risks associated with this strategy.

While all of the chapters in this book are important to beginners, chapter eight is often one of the most used chapters in any beginner's guide. This chapter focuses on a variety of tips for beginners. These tips come from other experienced traders who, through their blogs, articles, or books, wanted to give you helpful information so you can become a successful swing trader. This chapter will discuss tips such as joining an online community, making education a top priority, becoming flexible, and making sure you have the right mindset.

Of course, because I took time to discuss tips for beginners, I also wanted to make sure you received a good amount of information regarding mistakes that other swing traders have shared. While there are countless mistakes that swing traders make, it is part of the job and something that will never go away, I only discuss a few mistakes. A couple of the mistakes that I will look at are how many new traders have unrealistic expectations about swing trading and how many don't pay attention to their mental health.

Through my research for this book, I came across and educational site about swing trading which discussed the 11 commandments of swing trading. As I was reading through these commandments, I realized that this is some of the most valuable information I had read about the topic. Therefore, I included this in the book. Some of the commandments are how you always make sure to have a clear plan, you need to work to put the odds in your favor, and you always need to remember to look at long-term charts.

In trading, there are two main forms of analysis. The first one is fundamental analysis, which I discuss in chapter eleven. This chapter focuses on a variety of fundamental valuables that you can use when you are analyzing and explains what fundamental analysis is. The second form of analysis is called technical analysis. This is the bigger form of analysis between the two, which means that this book focuses more on technical analysis than fundamental analysis. When looking at technical analysis, which is chapter twelve, I explain what you will study through the technical analysis lens.

Chapter thirteen takes a look at how you can limit your risk as a swing trader. It is important to note that you will never be able to eliminate risk completely. However, you can use a variety of techniques in order to limit your risks as much as possible when you trade stocks. Some of the strategies I will focus on are how to keep your emotions in check, determining your stop-loss amount, how you shouldn't trade alone (especially as a beginner), and how you should follow the 1% rule.

Finally, chapter fourteen will look at how psychology and swing trading are important to each other. In this chapter, I will discuss how you need to focus on keeping mentally healthy, so you can become the best swing trader possible. For example, I will discuss how you need to make sure you get enough sleep, how you need to focus on the positive, and how you need to practice self-control.

Through all these chapters, you will receive

one of the most in-depth looks at swing trading on the market. You will not only learn what swing trading is, but you will also learn techniques, tips, and how psychology is a part of swing trading.

Chapter 1: Introduction to Financial Trading

While all the chapters of this book are equally important, it is important to start with this chapter because you get the basics of trading in general. What I mean is, you will want to read this chapter before you read any other chapter in this book. There are many people who will often skip to a chapter they feel they are interested in or need the most. For this book, it is important this is the first chapter you read, as it will prepare you for further reading.

At the base of financial trading is the hope that you make a profit through buying and selling stocks, currencies, or other commodities. There are many types of financial trading. This book focuses on swing trading, but there is also day trading, position trading, and momentum trading. While they each focus on the same basic idea of making a profit, they are all a little different in the trading world.

Before I go any farther, I should mention a myth about trading. This myth states that the only people who can take on trading as a profession are the people who have significant wealth. Fortunately, with today's technology, brokers who are willing to work with people who don't meet the $25,000 minimum balance rule and other factors, anyone can become a trader. While you can't open a trading account with no money, you do not need thousands of dollars to put into your account at first. You can start with a few thousand and then work your way up. If you are a trader who starts with only a few thousand, you will want to make sure that you find the best broker to work with you. Furthermore, you will want to make sure that the broker has relatively cheap fees.

Trading vs. Investing

Before you get into trading, you should know the difference between trading and investing. One reason I want to discuss this is because there are a lot of people who get into trading and realize it is different from investing. In reality, they wanted to start investing their money and not focus on trading. Another reason is because trading isn't for everyone. While anyone can take on trading, some people are more interested in investing. On top of this, there are people who don't have the patience to focus on trading or they find the job to be too stressful.

This is not to say that you need to decide right now if you are meant to be an investor or a trader. You should definitely look at all your options and even try out simulation trading before deciding. simulation trading is when you start to trade financial instruments but complete the process without money.

While investing is seen as a long-term approach to building your wealth, trading is seen as a short-term approach which allows you to maximize returns. Returns are the money that you will receive daily or during certain times of the year. In a sense, it is the income you have generated during trading.

Investors will often build their wealth by starting a retirement account or using the buy and hold stock method. One of the most popular buy and hold investors of 2019 is Warren Buffet, who became a millionaire through investing. Investors don't tend to pay attention to the daily trends of financial investments. For example, they will not decide to sell a stock because the price decreased. In fact, some investors don't pay attention to the daily price of stocks at all and, therefore, might not even realize the price of the stock decreased. If they do notice, they don't worry about it because they know that the price will increase over time. It is important to note that you might already be an investor. Anyone who pays into a 401K or has a savings account is considered to be an investor.

Traders build their wealth by purchasing and selling stocks over a short period of time. Day traders will buy commodities in the morning and then sell them at the best opportunity they see that same day. Swing traders will hold on to their financial instruments for a little longer. Sometimes they have them for a few days and other times up to a couple weeks. Another type of trader is known as a position trader, who tends to hold their instruments anywhere from a few months to a year or so. Scalp traders are similar to day traders in that they never hold their stocks overnight (which would turn them into swing stocks); however, they also don't hold the stock for most of the trading day. Instead, scalp traders will only hold their stocks from seconds and into a few minutes.

Key Concepts of Financial Trading

What Are You Trading?

One of the first questions you should ask yourself is what financial instruments, such as stocks, bonds, or ETFs are being traded. Even though you will always want the same outcome, which is a profit, you will want to make sure you understand the financial instrument that is being traded because you will handle each one differently.

Who is Doing the Trading?

This is an important question because you need to be able to identify the trader. You are the trader or is someone else doing the trading? You need to be able to identify the financial instrument part of a company, government institution, or person. This is important because you have to be able to identify the commodities which move the most. When this happens, they are known to be part of a volatile market which bring both positives and negatives. On the positive side, financial instruments from volatile markets will give you bigger capital gains, which is when you make a profit. On the other side, they also bring more risk.

Where Are You Completing the Trade?

There are two places where you can complete a trade. The first one is known as over-the-counter, which is like when you trade a CFD with an institution. The second place is known as an exchange, such as the New York Stock Exchange. These are often completed through an online marketplace.

How Are Stocks Traded?

The days of shares needing to be traded in the building of the New York Stock Exchange or London Stock Exchange are gone. While many people still work in these buildings, it is more common for people to take in over-the-counter stock exchanging. This type of exchanging is what you do when you sit in front of your computer and use a platform to buy and sell financial instruments. With this type of trading, everything you do is recorded electronically which is a huge advantage for any trader. Because of this, you are able to screenshot all of your transactions and make notes on them, so you can look back at them in the future. This is known as post-trading analysis and will be discussed later.

It is important to realize that when you buy a stock, you are not buying a stock directly from the company. You are buying the stock from the shareholder. The company sold the stock before you purchased the stock from the shareholder.

This is the exact same thing as when you sell a stock. You are not part of the company selling a stock, you are a shareholder who is selling the stock to the new shareholder.

Finding a Broker

While all traders won't have a broker, it is important that you find the right broker for you when you are starting your swing trading career. A broker is the person who will not only help you perform your trades, but will also give you an advice, reading material, help you with research, and help you in any other way he or she can as a broker.

The biggest rule when it comes to finding a broker is you have to find one that you can trust and respect. You need to remember, you will not only be giving this broker your important bank information, but you will start your new career alongside this broker. You will be getting advice, learning how to make trades, letting your broker help you decide what trades to make, and so much more.

There are different types of brokers.

1. Interactive Broker

Unfortunately, if you can't make the $25,000 minimum amount pattern day trader rule then you can't use an interactive broker. However, if you can make this rule, then you might want to look to see if this is the type of broker for you because they tend to be the cheapest with fees. For example, they usually only charge about $1 per trade, but they will have other fees associated with this amount which all brokers will have.

2. Sure Traders

Sure Traders are brokers who will help people who cannot make the pattern day trader rule. However, they also tend to be a little more expensive. On average, they charge about $10 trading fee and could charge other fees on top of this. Sure Traders are known to be some of the most helpful brokers for beginners, especially traders who take on the swing trading career.

3. Full-Service Brokers

Full-Service brokers are ones who many people feel go above and beyond their job. While they are not the most popular among traders, they are a great source of help for swing traders. They will often be the brokers you want to pick if you are more interested in learning as much as you can through your broker. Unfortunately, because they give the whole package with their service, they tend to be some of the most expensive brokers.

4. Discount Brokers

Discount brokers are similar to the interactive broker as they are known to be extremely cheap. However, they won't always work with traders who have under $25,000 in their account. Discount brokers also tend to specialize with traders and don't often work with people who are interested in investing for more than a couple of years.

Make Sure You Understand Your Rights

No matter how well you trust your broker, you should always remember that you have rights. There are several rights that many traders and investors are not aware of when it comes to their relationship with their broker. The following list is of the most important rights you should remember when you start working with your broker.

- You have the right to look up your broker's historical professional information. While you might have to call your county or state offices, you are guaranteed the right to know if your potential broker has been cited with any illegal activity or any other customers have filed a complaint against your broker.

- If your broker does not give you the information you request, you have the right to go to your broker's supervisor to request the information. If you still don't receive any information from the supervisor, you have the right to go above the supervisor to receive the information. This might mean that you go to the company's headquarters or you reach out to your state agency.

- You have the right to receive all reports and correspondence in writing.

- You have the right to understand all the trades your broker is making on your behalf. You also have the right to make the final decision when it comes to trading.

- You have the right to be informed of any new information that details your stocks and trading portfolio.

- You have the right to ask any questions, so you can completely understand all of the trading information which is given to you.

Bull vs Bear Market

There are dozens of new trading terms that you will learn along your journey and one of the most common terms are bull and bear. These terms are two types of markets which focus on the current conditions within the stock market. They will often help you in deciding if you should take on a trade or not.

Bull Market

When the conditions of the market are doing well, it is referred to as a bull market. This means that not only are the stock market trends on the rise, but unemployment is low, and most people tend to not struggle as much financially. For a trader, bull markets can make it easier to pick stocks because the majority of the stocks are doing well.

Even though the conditions are great when it comes to the bull market doesn't mean that there aren't dangers associated with this type of market. One of the biggest problems with bull markets is known as a bubble. What happens is things seem to be going so well with trading that many traders will over evaluate the positive conditions. Basically, the stock market prices get too high. This can cause the conditions to not follow in their traditional manner and soon the good conditions will burst.

Bear Market

The bear market is the exact opposite of the bull market. In a bear market, the conditions aren't great as unemployment will be high and the stock market trends will be on a downward spiral. The biggest problem for traders when it comes to a bear market is that it is riskier for them to take on stocks. Of course, this doesn't mean that they stop trading. Instead, they are just become more cautious of the stocks they pick and do their best to find ones that will turn a decent profit.

Some traders during this time might stick to blue-chip stocks. These are stocks that are shares from the most powerful companies you can think of today, such as Target, Walmart, Apple, Amazon, and Microsoft. However, if these aren't your targeted stocks or you are not comfortable taking on these types of stocks, it is best to remain in your comfort zone, especially during bear market conditions.

When faced with the bear market, most traders will do something called short selling. This is when they hold a stock for the shortest time possible as it will give them a more decent profit, or at least they won't lose as much money. With short selling, traders don't actually buy the stocks. Instead, they borrow the stocks and then sell them. Unfortunately, this can be very risky business for beginners. Furthermore, short selling carries its own set of risks.

One of the biggest reasons why short selling isn't meant for beginners is because it can become very tricky. In reality, you are often gambling with your money as you work towards trying to make a profit through borrowing and selling. There are very specific times that you need to find in order to short sell and make the best profit. Of course, any trader is able to accomplish short selling and become profitable. Like with any other factor in trading, you will just need to make sure that you do your research, speak with your advisor, and understand the process.

Chapter 2: What is Swing Trading?

Some people tend to confuse swing trading with other types of trading. It is important to know that each type of trading is different. For example, when you are a day trader, you will buy and sell stocks in one day. You do not hold stocks overnight. If you do decide to hold a stock overnight, you turn it into a swing trading stock. Swing traders tend to hold their stocks for a few days, however, they also have a limited time frame. While the average swing trader might hold on to stocks for a couple of weeks, some might hold on to stocks for as long as a couple of months. Typically, if a trade is held longer than this, it isn't considered a swing trade anymore. However, there are always exceptions to every rule.

Why Swing Trading Over Day Trading?

While you can take up any type of trading, many people feel that swing trading is better than day trading. Lately, day trading has become a popular topic because it can be completed within a few minutes to an hour or so. However, this is also one reason that people tend to turn away from day trading.

Other than the different time frames between day trading and swing trading, many people chose swing trading because they feel it is less demanding. There is a lot of truth to this as day traders often feel a bit more stress as they have to pay such close attention to the stocks in order to trade them in just the right moment, which can be within minutes, in order to make the best profit. While everyone has to focus on just the right moment to trade so they receive the best profit, day traders need to close out their stocks the same day they purchase them, otherwise they will most likely lose money.

Furthermore, day traders have to watch several screens throughout the day. Of course, much of this depends on how many stocks they take on. However, this tends to become very challenging, especially for beginners. When it comes to swing traders, they have to watch several screens closely, but not to the intensity of day traders.

Another reason people chose swing trading over day trading is that it's easier to be a part-time trader. While there are part-time day traders, many feel that it is a full-time job if you want to gain the best profits from the career.

When it comes to swing trading, you are given a few days and up to a couple of months to watch your stocks and find the best time to make your highest profit. Because of this, people don't feel as much pressure.

Swing traders also don't have to worry about making sure they have the greatest equipment and worry about all the algorithms that go into day trading. Instead, swing traders can get a platform and perform their own trades, once they learn, on a typical computer. Of course, you will still need to make sure that your computer is reliable and have the same high-speed internet that day traders need.

Stock Trends

Like with other types of trading, you will need to heavily focus on analysis in order to try to gain an idea of where the stock trend is heading next. For example, if you look at a stock's trend history for the last couple of months and noticed it has been in an upward trend, you might assume that this upward trend is going to continue. However, you will also need to look at other features in order to officially determine if this is the best stock for you. Thankfully, trends tend to repeat themselves which is why people can easily predict where the stock is going to go. However, this doesn't mean that trends don't quickly change.

There are times during an upward trend when you will see what traders call a pull-back. This is when the trend of the stock drops down but then rises back up later. Pull-backs also repeat. However, if they are successful, they will have higher lows and higher highs than the previous pull back.

This is a pattern that you will want to notice as a swing trader because, as long as the stock will work with your strategy and everything else matches up with your trading plan, it is the trend you want to find. The best time to buy one of these stocks is when is during a pull-back. This is when the stock will be at a low price, which means your profit will be greater, once the stock shoots up to a higher price and you can sell it at the right time.

Another type of trend that you have to understand as a trader is the downward trend.

This trend is the opposite of the upward trend but still can give you a profit, if you understand when to buy and sell the stocks. The best time to buy the stock on a downward trend is when the stock is at a low point. Of course, you will want to sell the stock when it is on its way back up from the lowest point, a term which is known as pull-up.

While this might sound pretty simple, it can actually be a little harder to understand and find the best time to buy and sell. The biggest way you will find the best time to buy and sell the stock is through technical analysis, which I will discuss later in this book. The basis of technical analysis is you will be able to identify the patterns because you analyze the historical trend and information of the stock. Through technical analysis, you will receive tools that will help you isolate and identify the patterns.

How to Decide on the Right Stocks

One of the most difficult decisions you will run into as a swing trader, or any trader, is deciding what stocks are the best to trade. There are a lot of factors that go into this from the strategies you use to your lifestyle. Unfortunately, I cannot give you a guide that strictly tells you what stocks you should go out and take on. However, I will try to give you information that can help you make your own decision.

One of the key features to look at when you are choosing your stock is to find a stock that comes from a large capital company. These companies might be part of the blue-chip stocks, such as Amazon and Walmart. However, they don't have to be. In general, large capital companies tend to have at least $5 billion dollars. These stocks are generally the most sought-after stocks in the market, which help make them highly tradable. They are also known to give you a good profit because they have a long history of success.

The trend is another key feature that you want to pay attention to. You want to make sure that the stock has been going in the same direction for a few days, if not a few weeks. This will help you to note that, chances are, the stock will continue this trend. Of course, if you decide to take on the stock, you want to continue to closely watch the stock because you never truly know when the stock will switch directions and you can find yourself losing capital instead of gaining.

Ideas on Good Swing Trading Stocks

While I cannot tell you exactly what stocks to get, I can give you an idea, so you can at least start to look at some stocks that many swing traders put into their basket.

Netflix

Netflix is considered to be one of the top swing trade stocks for 2019. Of course, this stock has a higher price than most swing trade stocks, which is often harder for beginners to take advantage of. However, if you have enough finances to put into Netflix, many traders feel it is a good option. Furthermore, because of the successful history of Netflix, many people believe that the stock isn't going to see a huge downward trend anytime soon.

Amazon

Amazon is similar to Netflix. It is believed to be one of the biggest swing trading stocks for 2019 because of its successful history. Like Netflix, Amazon is also on the more expensive side, however is known to give great returns.

MKS Instruments

In 2019, most tech companies are some of the top stocks that people take on as swing traders, day traders, and investors. MKS Instruments is based out of Massachusetts and has been on an upward trend for a while.

Chapter 3: Finding a Suitable Market

One of the most difficult parts of swing trading, especially for a beginner, is finding the best market for you. This includes what type of financial instruments you want to focus on when it comes to trading. There are a variety of financial instruments; such as ETFs, futures, options, currencies, cryptocurrencies, and stocks. As a beginner, it is important to try to find one financial instrument that you are comfortable with. This chapter will go into the different types of financial instruments, so you can gain a better sense of which instrument is the best for your trading lifestyle. While discussing the various types of financial instruments, I will also give you some of the pros and cons that go with these instruments. The goal for this chapter is to help you decide whether you are going to focus on stock, currencies, ETFs, or other another financial instrument.

Of course, while you want to pick one financial instrument, this does not mean that you can't do more research to see if you have chosen the right instrument. For example, you might feel that stocks are your best option because you hear the most about them. However, once you start to trading with stocks, you begin to think that you might be better of trading currencies. You can then switch your financial instrument to see if currencies are a better fit for you.

Sometimes, following the guideline of trial and error is the best way to help you develop yourself as a trader. It is important to realize that you should establish your own trading personality. While you will follow the advice of others, such as people in your online community and your broker, you should still make sure to take time to figure out what is right for you. Many beginners have felt uncomfortable as a swing trader because they were following what other traders were doing instead of learning about their trading personality. If you want to become a successful swing trader, you will focus on developing your trading personality instead of following someone else.

Selecting a Financial Instrument to Trade

Stocks

Stock are probably the most common financial instrument that people think of when they start their trading career. In fact, most people probably believe that this is the financial instrument they will be trading. Part of this is because of the popularity. However, another part is because they really don't realize how many financial instruments there are when it comes to trading.

When people talk about stocks in the trading community, they will often refer to them as shares. There are several ways you can handle shares. Of course, you can decide to trade shares using the swing trading technique or you can decide to invest your stocks with the buy and hold method. Whatever you choose to do (you might change your mind once you truly start trading) it is important to remember that you need to continue your research and get to know as much as possible about trading stocks in the market. This not only means that you have to learn about stocks, but it also means that you have to learn about the stock market in general.

In reality, this goes for any type of financial instrument you decide to focus on.

Because stocks are so popular, it is important to look carefully at your research. For example, you might find valuable information about a stock but realize the website is focusing on investing stocks instead of trading them. While you can learn about the details of a stock through this resource, you won't want to spend your time focusing on investing stocks when you are looking into trading. The main reason for this is because, as I have mentioned earlier, trading and investing are two different pieces of the stock market. When you invest, you hold the stock for a long period of time. In fact, there are many investors who focus on holding the stock for the rest of their life. But, when you are a swing trader, there is only a small window of time you will hold your stock. Therefore, you want to make sure that you are reading about the correct strategies and information to help you along your swing trading journey.

One of the biggest examples of running into information about stocks that won't be important to you as a swing trader is reading that you should not pay attention to the daily prices of the stock market. While this is valuable information for an investor who focuses on the buy and hold strategy, this is not valuable information for someone who is taking on swing trading. While you won't need to focus on every single price dip and rise like day traders do, unless you are trying to analyze a chart, you will need to pay close attention to the daily stock prices you have in your portfolio.

At the same time, you want to make sure that you are focusing on stocks that are within your target companies. For example, you might want to focus on blue-chip stocks. Therefore, if you find a stock that isn't considered blue-chip, you will want to move on.

One of the biggest downsides to choosing stocks is that each stock you take on will carry its own individual risk. This means that no matter what type of negative news comes about the company for a stock you hold, such as Google or Twitter, you will have the risk of losing money due to the negative news. However, there is a way to trade stocks without having to think of each stock carrying it's own risk and this is through ETFs.

ETFs

ETFs are known as Exchange-Traded Funds. When you think of ETFs you can picture a bunch of stocks in one basket. What this group of stocks or other securities you decide to trade do is analyze the underlying index of the fund. There are a variety of ETFs. For example, you can choose an ETF that follows more of a target, such as retail companies or you could choose an ETF that has more variety within its basket. While you are looking at different ETFs, you want to keep in mind the same rules and guidelines for yourself that you do for stocks or any other type of financial instrument. While ETFs used to be focused more towards stocks, they can now focus on bonds, currencies, and even looking into cryptocurrencies.

One of the biggest pros to ETFs is you are able to have variety through purchasing one ETF because it is made up of different securities. Many people believe that this can save you money because if you decided to purchase the stocks in the ETF separately, you would be spending more money. For example, if you are interested in stocks that focus on space, you can look for an ETF that has this target instead of having to purchase a dozen or more separate stocks. In fact, most ETFs can hold hundreds of stocks.

Another positive of ETFs is you don't have to worry so much if one of the company's securities start to fall because of negative press as the other securities will help balance out the fall. Therefore, you might not even notice that price drop from one security. Because of this, many traders feel that ETFs are a good risk management instrument.

The price also tends to be more of a positive when it comes to ETFs. While most people believe that they will be expensive because they hold so many securities from different companies, this method of thinking isn't true. In fact, you might find that many ETFs are cheaper than some of the most popular blue-chip stocks on the market. On top of this, some ETFs might have a blue-chip stock within them.

Diversification is one of the terms that you will often run into as a trader. Diversification basically means that you have a variety of stock or whatever type of financial instrument you decide to trade. This is another reason why many traders look at ETFs as they will offer diversification through their variety of stocks.

However, many traders and investors feel that diversification can also be a negative in the stock world. While it is highly debated, some people feel that if you have too much diversification in your account, then you can find yourself struggling to manage some risks.

Currencies

Trading currencies is just like trading money when you go on a vacation. For example, if you live in Canada and you decide to travel to Europe, you will have to trade your Canadian money in for Euros. In a sense, trading currencies in the stock market works the same way. You will always need to have two different currencies in order to trade. You will also want to watch to see what the value of the money is through a comparison. For example, some currencies receive a higher value compared to others while other currencies receive a lower value.

Currency trades are completed in the Foreign Exchange Market, which is known as forex. While this is a different market, you will still want to make sure to follow the same risk management techniques that you do when trading in the stock market. For example, you will want to make sure that you only trade a certain percentage of your account amount, such as 1% (this will be discussed later). You will also want to make sure that you take all the time you need in order to learn about trading currencies and the foreign exchange stock market.

One important piece of advice from many experienced swing traders is that most of them agree that you should not start out trading using currencies as your financial instrument. They really believe that after you use simulation trading, you should turn your attention to stocks as these are often considered to be a base in the trading world. Stocks have been around an incredibly long time, which often helps beginners as they are learning the guidelines, rules, and how to trade in general.

Cryptocurrencies

Cryptocurrencies are one of the newest types of financial instruments available to trade. They are similar to currencies, however they are often discussed as coins and have a variety of different coins. Some of the types of cryptocurrencies are Ethereum, Ripple, Bitcoin Lite, and Bitcoin.

Just like currencies, nearly every experienced trader will tell you that beginners should not start with cryptocurrencies. In fact, most would probably see a beginner start with currency over cryptocurrencies. There are a couple main reasons for this one, both of them dealing with how risky these types of financial instruments are.

First, cryptocurrencies are newer and this means that there isn't as much research completed on them. In fact, one of the main things that experienced traders who are including cryptocurrencies in their portfolio are working hard to make sure they note everything about their trades so they can help expand the research on this type of financial instrument.

Second, cryptocurrencies are known to have high risk. In fact, many believe that they are the most high risk financial instruments that you can trade and invest in. They tend to suffer more than any other instrument when it comes to negative press, governmental regulations, and are even more likely to be hacked. Because of this, many traders feel it is important that the people who take on cryptocurrencies are comfortable with high risk, won't allow their mental state to be affected by the risk, and can remain calm under stress so they can continue to think rationally when having to make a quick decision to trade.

Futures

Futures are a good way to start your trading career. This is one of the most popular financial instruments among day traders but are also great for beginners who are looking to become swing traders. When you think of a future, you can think of an agreement between two people. A future is basically a contract that states exactly when stock will be sold. Typically, the agreement states that the stock will only be sold at a specific price. For example, both parties could agree that if the stock reaches $5, then the stock is to be sold. However, the stock cannot be sold to the second party until the price of $5 is reached.

Many people feel that futures are a great way to learn about the stock market. It decreases risk because you are able to create a contract that states this stock will be sold at a certain price. Of course, before you decide to agree to the contract, you will do all the research you need to do and make sure, to the best of your abilities, that you will end up with capital gain instead of a loss with the price you choose. Many beginners who state that they used futures within their first couple of months as a trader say they were able to get some more hands-on experience and learn about the stock market as they took part in futures. On top of that, they were able to gain pretty good profits.

Options

In the basic sense, options are similar to futures in there is a contract between two parties that states when the stock can be sold. However, instead of just focusing on the price, the agreement also focuses on a specific date. Furthermore, in order for the stock to become an option, there are four requirements that are needed.

1. The owner of the stock needs to agree upon the price. This process is known as the strike price.

2. You need to know the stock that the option is being applied to, such as IBM or MasterCard.

3. When it comes to options, buying is referred to as call and selling is referred to as put.

4. You also need to have a date of expiration for the option.

Like with any other type of financial instrument, there are positives and negatives associated with options. It is important to remember that all trades carry some sort of risk, no matter how well you try to manage the risk. This means that you can exhaust yourself making sure you have used every risk management technique that you can use and still have an amount of risk involved. Therefore, it is best to understand that sometimes you will lose on a trade and other times you will profit.

One negative side to options is the expiration date. If you hit the expiration date, then the agreement is considered to be worthless and you have taken a 100% loss on the stock. However, one of the positives of options is that you don't have to use a lot of capital in order to trade a high priced stock.

Chapter 4: Treat Swing Trading Like a Business

One of the most important pieces of information to receive as you start on your journey is that you will become more successful as a swing trader if you treat it as a career and not just a hobby. You don't have to work full-time in order to believe that swing trading is a profession to be taken seriously. Some traders decide to work part-time because this is best for their lifestyle. For example, a stay-at-home parent will often become too distracted to focus on trading the whole day. When you take on trading full-time, you will usually be in front of your computer during the hours the New York Stock Exchange is open, which is about 9:30 am to around 4:00 pm Eastern time zone. This means, if you live in California, then you will start your day before 6:30.

Establish Your Business Plan

Because you should treat trading like a profession, it is important to follow a number of steps you would use when starting your own business. First, you will want to make sure you create a business or trading plan. This is a plan which will discuss all the details about your style as a trader. You will discuss your enter strategy, exit strategy, your pre-trading analysis, and your post-trading analysis.

What is a Business Plan?

Your business plan is going to be your comprehensive guide that will help you with your decisions as a swing trader. These are not only important because every business should have one but because they can help you make the best decision when you are faced with deciding if you should take on or sell a financial instrument. No matter how well you have researched swing trading or how long you have been a swing trader, when you are faced with a decision you can easily struggle to come up with a solution. This is when your trading plan will come in handy. You will focus on every aspect that goes with swing trading, including tips to help you focus on making the right decision and why.

It is important to evaluate your trading plan often. In fact, many traders state you should read through your trading plan during your pre-trading analysis. Other traders state that you should at least read through your plan and make any changes, if necessary, on a weekly basis. Whatever you decide to do, you want to make sure that you know your trading plan as well as you know anything else in trading. Even though you will be reading the plan often, you still want to make sure you have memorized the plan as this will help you when you are faced with a difficult decision.

Why You Need a Trading Plan?

Your trading plan has several advantages. First, it will help you make decisions when you are focusing on a trade. While you might feel that these decisions should be easy, there is a lot of analyzing and details that go into making a decision to take on a financial instrument. This means that when you are faced with a decision that you need to make within a minute or two, you can often become stressed or worried about your decision. Of course, this isn't something you want to do when it comes to trading as then you might make the decision with your emotions, which definitely isn't something you want to do as a trader. If you find yourself in this position, you can turn to your trading plan. This plan will walk you through your decision, so you are less likely to make any mistakes.

Set Your Schedule and Stick to It

I talk about establishing your schedule, I am not just talking about how long you will sit in front of your computer when you are trading. There is a lot of information which goes into creating your schedule.

First, you will want to decide if you are going to become a part-time or full-time swing trader. This will let you know how much time to set aside for your trading career. For example, if you are part-time, you might think about focusing on trading a couple of days during the week or trade in the mornings. However, if you are a full-time trader, you will probably want to stay close to your computer during the hours the stock market is open. Below are the pieces of your schedule you should make sure to include no matter how often you trade during the week.

Pre-Trading Analysis

You will want to make sure to include time for your pre-trading analysis, which is a part of your trading plan. This analysis typically takes place before the stock market opens; however, some traders will use the first half hour as their analysis time. For instance, if you want to make sure your analysis is complete by the time the stock market opens, you will want to make sure you are done with this part of your day by 9:30 Eastern time. This could mean that you start your day at 5:45 am or 6:00 am as it is a good idea to have at least a half hour for your pre-trading analysis. However, many traders state that beginners should allow themselves a bit more time because they are still learning the whole trading system. Therefore, it could take them more time to analyze the changes that occurred in the foreign stock market or the United States stock market overnight. On top of this, they might take more time reading the news.

The Market

Of course, you will want to make sure that your schedule includes the on goings of the stock market. For example, you will want to note that from about 9:30 am to around 10:00 am, the market is in volatile mode. This means that there are a lot of changes occurring in the market which makes it unstable. When the market is unstable, you typically do not want to make and purchases or sales. Most people tend to just sit back and watch the market or spend their time reading the news or doing some research.

Another time to note about the stock market is that from about 11:15 am to around 2:00 pm is when the market seems to have the lowest amount of activity. Many traders refer to this time as the stock market's lunch time. Before 11:00 am, many traders will end their day as they are only part-time. However, those who are full-time might continue to research or look for stocks until their lunch time.

Starting around 2:30 pm, the stock market will begin to pick up again. When this happens, you will start to see activity and, if you are planning on making a sale or trade, you will most likely start looking into that. This activity continues until the stock market closes around 4:00 pm.

Post-Trading Analysis

Post-trading analysis is just as important as pre-trading analysis. You want to make sure to make time for this every day and it will occur after you have completed your day. During your post trade analysis, you will reflect on your day and you can do this through a trading journal or by taking screenshots of your charts for any trades you made that day.

If you use a trading journal, you will want to make sure to note every detail you feel is necessary about the day. This not only includes any financial instruments you bought or sold but also why. You will want to focus on why you made the decision, what strategy you used, what factors contributed to this decision, you will want to discuss if you were distracted, what device you used (computer, phone, etc.), your capital gain or loss, and anything else. It is important to write down as much as you feel you will need to so when you can get a sense of where your strengths and weaknesses are. On top of this, you will be able to get to know yourself as a trader.

If you decide to take screenshots of your charts, you will want to make sure to make notes within your charts. You will want to find a spot where you won't become distracted and can still read the chart easily. You will want to make the same type of notes you do in your trading journal. Of course, you could always take screenshots of charts and also keep a trading journal. How you do your analysis is up to you.

Take Your New Career Seriously but Not Too Seriously

Before you get into swing trading, whether you are going to focus on it halftime or full-time, you want to make sure that you are 100% committed to the career. It is very important that you don't feel like this is something you just want to try because you are bored or want to see if you can make some extra money every month. However, if you do feel this way, it is best to start up part-time and go from there.

At the same time, you need to make sure that you don't fall into the trap of taking your job too seriously. While this might sound odd, it can happen and has happened to many people within their jobs. Typically, when people start taking their job too seriously, they start to let it consume their life and there is very little professional and personal life balance. In fact, what happens is people tend to put all their time and energy into their job that they reach a state of exhaustion.

Becoming exhausted from trading can happen to anyone, and it is a fairly common trait, especially for beginners. Part of this reason is because they don't understand how demanding trading really is. Therefore, when they first get into the business, they have not dedicated enough time for what they wanted to do. Of course, this can be easily fixed by creating more time for trading or taking on less stocks. But, at the same time, they could reach a state of exhaustion before they realize they took on too much.

How to Tell When You're Heading Towards a Burn-Out?

Becoming burned-out from you job can happen to anyone. In fact, most people feel that they reach a stage of burnout at least once throughout their professional career. It is important to note that if you start to feel burnt-out, it is best to take a step back or a break. If you continue to work at the pace you are going and become too exhausted, you can easily start to cause other work-related problems. For example, you can start performing poorly. When it comes to swing trading, you might find yourself making more mistakes and unable to read and analyze charts that you used to be able to understand easily.

Many people reach a state of burn-out simply because they feel their job is too stressful. In fact, stress is the main factor of becoming burned-out. This is a common problem for many people in the trading community because, even swing trading, can be demanding.

There are many basic signs for a person who is starting to become burnt-out from there job.

1. You have lost your motivation for your job.

One of the biggest signs that you are nearing or becoming burnt-out is you have lost motivation for your job. This can happen to any one and in any field, not just trading. In fact, you might have already felt this way in a previous job. When you lose motivation, you really begin to feel that you can't do the tasks that you once used to do. You might feel that you are too tired to perform the tasks (exhaustion is another sign of being burned-out). You might also feel that the tasks aren't worth your time or find yourself procrastinating.

2. You feel a lot of negative emotions.

Another sign that you are becoming burned-out is you feel more negatively towards your job than positively. You might find that you are easily irritated by your co-workers or even feel that you just want to be left alone. You might find yourself becoming easily frustrated at the simplest tasks you need to complete. Of course, you will want to remember that people generally feel a bit negative about parts of their job from time to time. If you find yourself feeling negatively occasionally, you might not be burnt-out. However, if you notice that you are more negative than you typically are, especially if you begin to become concerned over your mental health, then you are most likely burn-out.

3. Your job performance is suffering.

One of the biggest ways to notice that you are burnt-out is by looking at your previous job performance and comparing it to your current performance. If you found your performance is sloppier and you are not putting as much effort into your job duties, then you have most likely become burned-out.

4. Always thinking about work, even when you're not working.

While people usually think about the things they need to do at work when they are not on the clock, if you find yourself doing this often you could easily be at the burnt-out stage. In fact, part of the reason you might feel burned-out is because you think of your job when you should be focusing on other things to give yourself a better balance between work and home.

This is one downside when it comes to working from home. People who are used to working in an office and then start to work from home can often find themselves working longer hours or thinking about work more. One reason for this is because it's more convenient for them to get to their office as it might just be down the hall. Furthermore, if you are a trader, you might trade through your desktop, which you use throughout your day for various reasons. This is why it is important to make sure you have some type of work schedule that you stick to when you work from home.

5. Your mental health is starting to decline.

Your mental health is one of the most important factors of your life. It is just as important as your physical health. In fact, it's been proven through scientific studies that if you're struggling with your mental health, you can become sick more often. Because your health is so important, you have to make sure to keep your mental health as healthy as possible. In order to do this, you have to watch for any signs of feeling burned-out. Unfortunately, once your mental health start to decline you have felt burned-out for a while.

Once you start to notice yourself struggling with your mental health, you can quickly run into other concerns, such as anxiety and depression. You start to take less care of yourself. For example, you might feel that you don't have to eat healthy when you typically watch what you eat. You might also stop exercising as you just don't feel like it anymore. It is important to note that if you start to feel this way, you should take a break from your job as quickly as possible. Even taking a couple of days or a week off can help you feel better about yourself and set your motivation back on track.

Chapter 5: Learning the Art of Swing Trading

The foundation of this chapter is to learn how to enter into the world of swing trading. However, before I get into actually learning about swing trading, it is important for you to remember a few basic points.

First, while swing trading is easy, you will probably find it a bit harder at the beginning. This should not make you feel that you cannot handle swing trading. However, it should help you realize that you will need to take time and continue to research and learn from others about the career of swing trading.

Second, even the most experienced swing traders make mistakes. There is no perfect guide when it comes to swing trading. You're going to make mistakes and will probably make more mistakes than some of the swing traders you know because you are just getting your start in the field. You should never let this deter you from becoming a successful swing trader. While some mistakes might make you lose more money than you thought, you should continue to learn from your mistakes as this will help you become more successful in the future. On top of this, you could become one of the next experienced swing traders who create their own website or book in hopes of helping beginners learn the art of swing trading.

Step 1: Start with Research

Throughout this book, you will read a lot about how research is important when you start getting into the field of swing trading. Of course, no matter what trading or investing you decide to do, you will always want to make sure to do your research and learn as much as you can about the topic. This is not only going to include website that you can find through a Google search, but also books from Amazon or your local library, and online classes. On top of this, you will want to join some online communities about swing trading, so you can get to know other swing traders and allow them to help you along your journey. It is important to note that swing traders aren't in competition with each other. Instead, when it comes to trading the person you are in competition with is yourself. When it comes to other swing traders, they want to do what they can to help you become successful. Therefore, online communities are a great resource when it comes to learning the trade.

Of course, before you start researching the topic, you will want to make sure you understand the basics of research. While you might have spent time in school researching for a few papers, this research will be more in-depth than other forms of research.

Tips to Help You Increase Your Research Skills

1. Start with Wikipedia – but don't use it as a source.

There is a lot of controversy around Wikipedia. There are people who believe that Wikipedia is one of the greatest websites to help you with your research and there are people who believe you shouldn't go near it if you are researching. However, when it comes to trading, Wikipedia is a great resource to start with. Not only can you get a general idea of what the topic is about, as people tend to easily explain things in Wikipedia, but you can also get a variety of websites from the list of citations at the end of the article.

In fact, no matter where you go to find your research, it is always a good idea to check some of the resources for that source. Not only will this help you confirm what the article is saying, but it can lead you to more educational or reliable sources.

2. Always make sure your source is reliable.

When it comes to research, a reliable source is the most important source you can find. There are many forms of reliable sources from government websites to people who are experts on the topic. Once you start researching and get an idea of what the topic is about, you will quickly be able to pick up the more reliable sources.

3. Look at your research like it is a puzzle.

One of the best ways to research is learn about one piece of your topic at a time. In a sense, you can look at your whole research topic as a puzzle you need to piece together. You start with one piece and then you move on to the next piece. You continue this process until your puzzle is completed. You can handle research the same way. You can first start by making a list of all the areas within your topic and then begin researching these sections one by one. As you research, you can make notes and write down ideas which can sometimes lead you in a better direction in your research.

4. Keep track of your sources.

One of the biggest mistakes that a lot of people make when they start researching is they don't keep track of their sources. There are a lot of ways that you can create a list of sources. For example, you can make a word document that holds the URL's from the internet sources you used. You could also make a bibliography which lists all the information about the sources.

5. You will need to be patient.

Unfortunately, you won't always find the information you need exactly when you want it. For example, there are times you might spend three hours researching the topic and barely find any information that you consider useful about your section. But, there will also be times where you research for a couple of hours and you find more resources that you thought you were going to.

6. Be consistent with your schedule and process.

Just as you will treat your new trading career as a profession, you want to do the same thing when it comes to researching for your new job. You will want to make sure you set time throughout your day for research. You will also want to make sure that you create a system and you keep using your system every time you work on your research. Doing this will be able to keep you more organized. On top of that, you will be able to understand what you are reading and learning better as you will have a clearer mind.

Step 2: Find a Broker

Because we already discussed the importance of not only finding a trusted broker but also knowing what your rights are, I am not going to go into that again. However, finding a broker is one of the early steps when you are getting into swing trading, therefore, it deserved a place on this list.

Once you find a broker, he or she will help you get started with setting up your account. On top of this, your broker will continue to help you with research, give you any advice you need, and answer any questions you have. This is another reason why it is important to find a broker early. It is always a good idea to have a like-minded individual that you can talk to about swing trading.

Step 3: Simulation Trading

After you start working with your broker, the next step is to look into simulation trading. While your broker should advise you to start your trading career with simulation trading, if he or she does not, then you should bring it up. With simulation trading, you will be able to get a real-time idea of what swing trading is like. The biggest plus of this is that you won't be losing any money if you make a mistake.

One of the biggest reasons you need to focus on simulation trading is because this will allow you to put your strategies and everything you have learned into practice. You will be able to find your strengths and weaknesses. On top of this, you can also make mistakes and find ways to learn from them, so you don't continue to make the mistakes in the future.

Another reason simulation trading is important is because it will allow you to start to get a sense of what trading is really like. No matter how much research you perform on swing trading, you will never truly be able to understand what the stock market and trading is actually like until you start to trade in real-time.

Step 4: Make Swing Trading Your New Career

Once you feel comfortable about trading. You can then start to look into working into trading with money. Once this happens, your days will start to become more like a career. Chances are you won't be working at swing trading full time during simulation trading, thought you could. However, once you start to get into trading with money, your days will become more consistent with the hours of the stock market.

A Swing Trader's Day

Pre-Trading Analysis

Your whole day at the stock market is going to be important, however, your morning pre-trading analysis can quickly make or break your career as a trader. You will want to take time before the stock market opens, which is 9:30 Eastern time, to get ready for the day, catch up on the news, see what change in the stock market overnight, and see how the foreign exchange market did. You can also use this time to see how your stocks are doing and scan the stock market to see what else catches your eye.

The Morning Stock Market

The New York Stock Exchange opens at 9:30 am, which means that you will have to adjust your time. For example, if you live in California, you will want to be ready for the stock market to open about 6:30 in the morning. This means that you will want to start your pre-trading analysis around 6:00 am or a little before, depending on how much time you take to analyze everything before the stock market opens.

It is important to note that for about the first half hour, the stock market is going to be very volatile. This means that there is going to be a lot of changes within the market and it will be unstable. Because of this, it is best to not make any move to sell or buy stocks. You want to let the market settle before you make any move. However, you can continue to scan the stock market to see if you can find your next interesting stock.

Once the volatile conditions slow down, usually around 10:10 in the morning, then you will start to see traders buying and selling. There will be a lot of day traders who are working on choosing their next best stock. On top of this, there will be a lot of other traders, including swing traders, who are thinking about buying and selling stocks.

Until around 10:30 am, you will find a lot of traders cashing out their trades. At this point, several of them will close out for the day. It is also around this time that you will start to see that stock market slowing down as people begin to get ready for lunch.

Lunch Time

When it comes to the stock market, the lunch time is between 11:00 am and 2:00 pm. During this time, the stock market is very quiet. If you are a full-time swing trader, this is around the time where you will not only grab lunch but also continue to work on research or just scan the stock market. You might also work on your afternoon plan. You won't be buying or selling very often during this time as there are not a lot of people taking part in the stock market.

The Afternoon Stock Market

Between 2:15 and 2:30 pm, you will start to see the stock market pick up again. This will happen because people are coming back from lunch and starting to get ready to close out the day. This means that the day traders will be quickly looking to sell all their stocks and swing traders will want to make sure that they are working on selling any stocks they need to at this point. As a swing trader, you might not sell and buy stocks every day. However, this doesn't mean that you won't be working. You will still want to take time to make sure that you keep up to date on the news, the information among the stock market, and your stocks.

In fact, the afternoon is a great time to start analyzing the stocks you have in your portfolio, especially if you have finished buying and selling any stocks you needed to for the day. You can spend this time looking at the trend lines and noticing what price your stocks sat at when the stock market opened, what the highest and lowest prices were. Furthermore, you can try to evaluate the stock and see if you can figure out the price the stock will close at. Doing this might help you gain more knowledge of how to analyze and establish a trend line, so you have an idea where it's heading to in the future.

About a half hour before the stock market closes, you will find that it becomes extremely busy again. This is the time where everyone is starting to close out for the day, which is exactly what you should be working on. If you have anything you have to close out, you will want to make sure to do this otherwise you can find that people will fill your orders without you realizing. When this happens, you can lose a lot of money. Therefore, if you have any orders that have not been filled, you must close them out before the end of the day.

After-Trading Analysis

Once the stock market officially closes about 4:00 pm Eastern time, you will be able to relax after a stressful day. On top of this, you will want to perform your after-trading analysis. This is when you take all the graphs you collected throughout the day from your trades, the current trades you hold, and start to analyze your graphs. While you are analyzing, you will want to pay attention to the trends and use the trends to follow a strategy to make sure you don't miss any details when it comes to analyzing your charts. In fact, many traders state that you should create a spreadsheet that lists everything you have to find during your after-trading analysis to make sure that you don't miss anything.

There are two basic ways that will help you record your after-trading analysis. One of these ways is to take a screenshot of all your charts and then makes notes in your charts. You will want to note the opening price, highest price, lowest price, and the closing price. On top of this, you will also want to make a note of any patterns you see in the trends, the conditions of the stock market, when you made the trade, why you decided to make the trade, and any distractions when you were making the trade.

Another way to help you keep up with your after-trading analysis is through having a trading journal. Similar to the charts, you will want to make sure to write down everything you can think of from your conditions at home to the conditions of the market. The reason why it is important to write down if you were distracted during a trade is because if you make a mistake, you can easily tell what might have caused you to make the mistake. For example, if you were making a trade and trying to feed your children at the same time, you might find that you should not complete both of these tasks at once. Instead, you will want to make sure that you have your time open when you need to take care of your children if you find them to be a distraction when it comes to trading.

One of the biggest reasons that you should keep a detailed analysis about your trading day, even if you just worked on research and didn't make a trade that day, is because you are able to analyze yourself as a trader. All experienced traders will tell you that everyone has a trading personality. Through how you handle the stock market, you will be able to find your strengths, weaknesses, and learn who you are as a trader. Of course, this can help you not only focus on building your strengths and turning your weaknesses into strengths, but it can also help you in finding target stocks for your investments or noticing when you are getting too emotional for the stock market.

Chapter 6: Trading Strategies

Like with any other version of trading, there are various strategies that you can use throughout your trading career. While most people like to stick to one or two strategies, which means they have to find financial instruments that work with their chosen strategies, other traders tend to go from one strategy to the next. However, as a beginner, it is best to realize that you should stick with one strategy as this will help you continue to learn about swing trading and how the stock market works in general. Of course, as you continue to build your trading knowledge and become more comfortable with swing trading, you can look into other strategies. While I cannot discuss all of the strategies in this chapter, I am discussing some of the most important and popular ones.

Trend Following

No matter what strategy you decide to use, you will need to make sure that you understand how to read charts and trend lines. You will use these tools in order to help guide you towards the best time to make your move to buy and sell a stock. When it comes to following a trend, there are a lot of details; such as what the opening price was, the highest price, the lowest price, and the closing price. You will analyze the trend over a period of time, how long depends on your personal preference. Through your analysis, you will start to notice a pattern in the trend line. This is the pattern that you will follow when you decide to take on a stock, see if your strategy will work for the stock, or what strategy to use.

The factors that you will look at when trend following are:

Price of the Stock

The price of the stock is one of the most important features that you will pay attention to. This doesn't just mean the price of the stock at that moment, such as what you would pay in order to purchase the stock. Even though the current price is the most important price, you will want to pay attention to all of the prices that you see for every day that you take into your analysis. For example, if you decide to look at the historical context of the last two months, you will look at about 60 days of stock pricing in order to help you find a trend. This means that you will look at the opening price for each of these days, the closing price, the highest price, and the lowest price. You will want to look at these prices in detail and in general. In a sense, this means that you will look at the larger image and the smaller pieces that make up the larger image.

Managing Your Money

Money management is thought to be one of the trickiest parts of trading. When it comes to managing your money, you want to make sure that you don't have too much money as it can give you a bigger loss. However, if you have too little money for the stock, then you aren't able to reach the full benefits when you make the trade. This is another time in swing trading when you want to find the best spot in order to make the trade.

One of the biggest tips to help you figure out how much money to put towards a stock is by evaluating the risks associated with the stock. You will be able to do this through any strategy that you will use and various other factors that are part of your trading plan.

Rules and Guidelines

One of the most important factors to remember when you are looking towards your trend line and thinking of making a trade. These rules are not only the guidelines that you will receive as you start to learn the swing trading technique, they are also the rules that you will set for yourself. For example, if you decide that your stop-loss price is going to be $10.00 lower than the price you bought the stock from, you will want to make sure that you follow this guideline.

One of the biggest reasons you need to make sure that you are following your guidelines is because the more consistent you are with your trading, the more likely you are to become successful. Furthermore, you will want to make sure that you follow the guidelines as they will help you to think systematically when it comes to making decisions. While you might find yourself turning back to your trading plan and guidelines consistently as a beginner, the more you follow the same procedures, the more you will focus on them as a way in making sure you are following the steps instead of needing them more for direct reference on where to go and what to do next. In a sense, trading will start to become more natural to you, which is a great strength when you are analyzing trend lines.

Diversity

Diversity is one of the more popular controversies when it comes to trading. While some traders feel you need to have great diversity, which is a variety of stocks, in your portfolio others feel that this isn't as important. In reality, the more serious you want to be with your trading, the more you will focus on diversity. However, this isn't always true when it comes to investors. But, as stated before, investing and trading are two different career paths in the stock market.

You can look at diversity as what is the right feature for you. You might find that you don't need to have a large diversity because you are a part-time swing trader or you have a specific target that you focus on. However, you might also find that the more diversity you have, the better-rounded you feel as a trader. You might find that diversity is helping you learn more about investing in general.

Always Note the Risk

Another important factor to pay attention to when you are looking into trend following is how much risk is involved if you decide to take on the financial instrument you are looking at. When you are looking at the risk, you always have to pay attention to your guidelines and your trading plan. These two factors will help you decide if you should take on the stock due to the risk it carries or not. It is important to remember you need to stick to the risk level you are comfortable with. Even if you think that this stock could give you good rewards, this doesn't mean that you should agree to take on the financial instrument if you are uncomfortable with the risk.

This also doesn't mean that you can't increase your risk level as time goes on. You just want to make sure that you build your confidence and comfort level with risk as your risk grows. Furthermore, as you get more knowledgeable with swing trading, it might be a good thing to slowly increase your risk when it comes to taking on stocks. It's always good to grow in many directions as a trader, including with risk.

Trend following tends to be one of the most popular techniques when it comes to trading because it has a high success rate, providing you understand where the trend line is heading. Of course, you should always remember that the stock market can take drastic turns and no one can truly predict the future. This means, even if you analyze the trend lines to the best degree, you will still have some risk involved as the trend line could differ a bit from what you originally thought.

Using Options as a Strategy

We have already discussed what options are; however, one factor I did not discuss is how options are usually seen as a strategy when it comes to trading. Because you are able to set up an agreement which gives you the option to buy or sell the stock later, you are technically strategizing the right time to take the next step in the future.

One of the biggest ways to do this is through analyzing the various charts that you see for your stock. In fact, you will focus a lot on technical analysis, which is something I will discuss later. You will focus on the historical charts of the stock as this will give you a time-frame for when you will want to take the next step.

Options are known to be a great strategy if you are looking for leverage, which is when you increase a return on a trade through borrowed money. It is important that you need to make sure you will only use this strategy if it will help you to receive more of a profit. In fact, this is one of the most important factors of choosing a strategy. You have to make sure that it is going to help you gain a profit and decrease your risks.

Short Interest

Many experienced traders state that beginners should not take part in the short interest strategy as it tends to be more of a guessing game than other strategies. When you focus on the short interest strategy, you will compare the number of short shares to the number of floating shares.

This is a great strategy to learn as a swing trader because it can show when the stock market is about to go into bearish conditions, which means that the stock prices will start to go down. Furthermore, short interest can also warn you about short squeezing.

Pay Attention to the Float

One of the best ways that you can tell if a trade is going to help you is through a technique known as float. Basically, a float is the total number of shares that a trader will find in public sharing. This can become very helpful because, if you have the right size of float, you can see higher profits.

However, this is also the trick when it comes to the float strategy. There tends to be a fine line between having a massive float and having a float that will give you the best profits. The reason why a massive float, which would be too many shares, can cause you to lose capital instead of increasing your profits is because if you have a huge float, the price won't move as quickly. However, if you have a smaller amount of shares in your float, then you will find that the price moves a bit higher, of course this gives you a larger profit. With this said, you also don't want to have too little shares in your float. If this happens, then you won't be able to make much of a profit either as this can stop your float from increasing in price.

Breakout and Breakdown Strategies

When you focus on the breakout strategy, you are looking at the history of your stock's trend line in a microscopic fashion. What I mean by this is you will be focusing on what the trend has done over the past few days. When you are looking at the trend line, you will see every time the price has gone up and down. Stock prices are almost constantly changing throughout the day, which is what the trend line shows. Every now and then, you will notice in the trend line that you have a several high points and several low points. These high points indicated the highest prices of the stock and the lowest points show the lowest prices.

The biggest difference between the breakout strategy compared to the breakdown strategy is the condition of the market. If you notice that the stock has been going on an upward trend for a while, you will use the breakout strategy. However, if you notice that the trend shows the price has been decreasing over time, you will use the breakdown strategy.

Of course, for both strategies, there is that specific spot you need to try in order to gain your best profit. The best spot to make your next move will depend on the pattern of the trend.

News Playing

As you know by now, one of the most important parts of your day is your pre-trading portion. This is one of the first things you will do once you start your day. You will want to do this before you start trading; however, you will probably be checking out the stock market so you can see the changes in your stocks and any target stocks that you are watching. However, one of the most important parts of this part of the day is reading the news that happened over night. This is important because you need to know what news is going to affect what stock, especially if you own the stock. You should always make note that any type of news can affect the pricing of financial instruments. For example, if you read that a company donated a large amount of money towards a nonprofit organization, people might be more likely to invest in that stock. However, if you read any negative news about a company, you will find the stock price going down because people are selling their shares.

But, you need to remember the trick of

keeping your emotions out of the stock market. While News Playing is a strategy which is used all across the board when it comes to the stock market, for example all traders and investors use this strategy, it is important to remember that you should never make a decision to sell or take on a stock because of your emotions. I won't go much more into this because I discuss how your emotions can be a risk factor in the stock market in another chapter, but it is also a big part of News Playing that you have to look out for.

You always want to make sure that you think logically when you are making a decision to buy or sell a stock. Even if you find you hold a stock where the price is dropping due to negative news, you want to make sure you continue to follow your trading plan instead of going on your emotions. Therefore, you should only focus on selling the stock if the price drops to your stop-loss price. You also should not hold on to a stock for longer than you originally planned, even if they are the center of a positive news story. While you can be a little flexible when the price continues to rise, at least in swing trading, you don't want to hold on to the stock for longer than a swing trader should. You always have to keep the time-frame in mind.

Chapter 7: The Art of Selling Short

One of the biggest pieces of advice you will hear from other traders is that you have to buy low and sell high if you want to make the best profit. This makes complete sense. Think about how retail markets work. Stores will often buy their stock at a lower price than what they sell them for. For example, the store owners might be able to purchase a notebook for $1.00 a piece, but when they put the notebook out on their shelves, they will most likely raise the price, which means you could be buying the notebooks for $1.50, which gives the store a .50 cent profit on each notebook they sell.

You want to think the same when you are trading stocks. You want to make sure that when you complete your trading plan for that particular stock that you set a stop-loss price as this will tell you how low you are willing to go. For example, if you decide that you don't want less than a dollar loss on a stock, you will set your stop-loss price at a dollar less than you paid for the stock. Of course, you hope that you will make a profit, which means that you will sell the stock at a higher price than what you paid for.

I have already discussed the difference between bull market and bear markets; however, to give you a bit of a review, a bull market occurs when the stock market is doing well and prices are rising. A bear market occurs when the stock market prices are dropping. So, when it comes to a bear market, you might ask why people trade as there isn't a way for them to make a profit. However, there is a way that traders can continue to make a profit when the stock market is seeing low numbers and this is through a technique called short selling.

How Short Selling Works

Unless you become a day trader, most traders will believe that they will hold on to their stock for a good period of time. Of course, when it comes to swing trading, you won't – or shouldn't – hold on to a stock for longer than a couple of months. With that stated, there are many beginning traders who feel that they are going to start trading and hold the stock for as long as possible as this will give them their best profit. If this is what you are thinking, you are looking more towards investing than trading.

The basic definition of short selling is when a trader takes on stock knowing that he or she is going to sell the stock after it has fallen in value. Of course, this is something that you are typically told not to do. However, there are many people who have used this position during bear markets and have found that it can be profitable. But, you are probably wondering how, if the price has lowered, the trader makes a profit from short selling. The truth of this trick is simple – the trader never actually takes ownership of the stock. Now your next question might be how a trader can sell a stock, and receive a profit, when he or she doesn't even own the stock. To look at this in a more basic way, let's look at it in two parts.

First, you have the part where the trader borrows the stock. This is usually done through a loan, which is similar to borrowing money from the bank. This means that the trader fully intends to buy the stock he sold back, which brings us to the second point. Because the stock prices continue to decline, the trader knows that he or she will be buying back the stock at a lower price than what they sold it for. Once they rebuy the stock, they send it back to the original owner, which closes out the loan, and the trader was able to make a bit of profit.

In order to start short selling, you will open a margin account through your broker. This account will use your profits in your account as collateral, just as a car is used as collateral for a vehicle loan. This means that if you are unable to repay your broker back in any way, your broker still receives the money as he or she can take it right out of your account. Furthermore, you need to note that you must be able to follow the 2:1 ratio when it comes to short selling. This means that your account must have at least 50% of what you are asking to borrow. For example, if you are asking to borrow $10,000 then you will have to have $5,000 in your account.

You need to be able to sell the stock to the first willing buyer. There isn't a huge time-frame for short selling. In fact, it tends to happen very quickly. Then, once the stock has sold, you have to go to the open market with that money and find a lower price for that stock. As you are doing this, it is important to remember that you have to buy back as many shares as you borrowed. Once you decide on your stocks, you will then inform your broker, who will make the transaction through your margin account. From there, your broker will receive his or her funds and you will receive the remaining profit.

The Risks of Short Selling

Of course, there are a lot of risk when it comes to short selling. The biggest risk is that you can never really tell the future. No matter how much you analyze charts or the general stock market conditions, such as if it's a bull or bear market, you will never be able to officially tell what a stock or the market is going to do. Because of this, one of your biggest risks is that you will have to buy back the stock at a higher price than what you sold it as. If this happens, you will take a loss instead of make the profit.

Another great risk when short selling is that you can get yourself into debt. Think of this – if you are unable to make a profit and you borrowed $20,000, this means you only have about $10,000 in your account. Therefore, not only will your broker take all the money in your account, but you still have to pay back the remaining $10,000.

Short selling is very strategic which can be risky, especially for a beginner. Short selling can seem like a very strange way to do things during an economic downturn. In fact, many beginners often question if short selling is even legal. Which it is, short selling is completely legal and is known to be a popular practice when the stock market is in bull conditions. However, because of its strategy and its risks, it can also be confusing for a beginner, even though you will be working with your broker.

Therefore, like with any other strategy, you want to make sure that you fully understand everything there is about short selling from the process to its risks before you decide to take on this technique during poor stock market conditions. While short selling occurs in a way that is meant to protect the trader's account, you also want to make sure that you understand that you can still bring yourself into debt if the process doesn't work as well as it should. You will also want to make sure that you go through the same trading plan, research, and following all your rules and guidelines before you decide to short sell. Understanding exactly what the stock market and the stock is doing will help limit your chance of a huge loss and, potentially, bringing yourself into debt.

Chapter 8: Tips for Beginners

Below are a variety of tips that you can carry with you into your new swing trading career. These tips are taken from experienced traders who want to give you the best advice that they can, so you can begin your new job with a positive mindset and feel ready to take on the swing trading world.

Learn from Your Mistakes and Move On

Successful traders learn several lessons early on in their career. One of these is mistakes are going to happen and when they do, you have to learn from it and move on. You cannot continue to hang on to the mistake you made as this won't help you psychologically. It is important as a trader to note that you should always be in the right frame of mind. When you start to dwell on your mistakes, then you are more likely to become emotional. This can allow your emotions to make decisions instead of thinking logically.

Even if you make a mistake that you read about on this list. This happens. You don't want to put too much stress on this mistake. Instead, you want to realize that you made the mistake, figure out what you can do so you are less likely to make the mistake in the future, and then move on.

Stay in the Right Mindset

Every successful swing trader knows that one of the most important pieces of the career is having the right mindset. The basis of this mindset is to believe that when you are confident in your abilities and you believe that you can become a successful swing trader, you will become a successful trader. There are a lot of parts to developing this mindset and it can take time, especially if you lack patience, confidence, and don't believe that you will be successful.

No matter where your mindset sits at this point, it will take time to develop the best mindset. When you work on creating this mindset, you want to focus on specific factors that will help boost your confidence. In return, you will start to believe in your abilities, start to feel that you will be successful, and then be able to hold this mindset throughout your career. It is important to note that in order to keep this mindset, you do have to remember that mistakes happen and not to take them too personally. As I stated before, learn from the mistakes and move on.

To help you develop and stay in the right mindset, you will want to follow a variety of techniques that I discuss throughout this book. For example, you want to follow your trading plan, remain flexible, realize mistakes happen, follow your schedule, keep your emotions in check, establish and evaluate your goals, and find the techniques and strategies that work for you.

Be Flexible

Many people get into the swing trading business with the belief that they have to follow the rules and guidelines exactly as they are written. On top of this, they believe that they have to make sure to follow their own rules exactly as they were created. In reality, when you become inflexible to the world of swing trading, including the rules, then you will start to feel stressed. This stress can put you in the wrong mindset for trading. For example, it can make you feel that you are not capable of becoming a successful trader.

While you want to follow the rules and guidelines, you should also remain flexible. First, you want to remember that life happens. Sometimes we plan to sit down to work but we have to go pick up a sick child from school or have a family emergency. When this happens, we might not be able to complete the financial instruments that we took on. This means that you will either keep them in your portfolio and take any loss or hope for a gain or you can trade them and close out for the day. When you are flexible, you will realize that this situation will be fine, and you won't dwell on the fact that you couldn't complete the job as you should have.

Remaining flexible will also help when you find yourself with unrealistic expectations, which is a common mistake among traders. On top of this, it will help you realize that mistakes happen and you shouldn't put too much emphasis on them.

Remember the Research

Learning is a common theme as a trader. It doesn't matter what type of trading you find yourself taking on, you will always want to make sure that you learn as much as you can before you start your career and continue to learn.

There are a variety of ways that you can focus on research and learning with swing trading. For example, reading this book is one way that you are researching and learning. You can continue to find other books that will help you along your swing trading journey. In fact, there are a variety of books on the topic that can help you. Some of these books I used for my research in this book while others I found along the way and thought I would include them in the following list.

Swing Trading: A Step By Step Guide To Trade Stocks, Forex And Options For Big Profits by Steve Arnold received publication in 2019 and is one of the newest books on the topic. This is a great book if you are interested in certain types of trading.

How To Swing Trade: A Beginner's Guide to Trading Tools, Money Management, Rules, Routines and Strategies of a Swing Trader by Brian Pezim and Andrew Aziz received publication in 2018. This is one of the most comprehensive books on the market about swing trading.

Swing Trading: A Beginner's Guide to Highly Profitable Swing Trades - Proven Strategies, Trading Tools, Rules, and Money

Management by Mark Lowe. This book is another one of the newest books on the market and is a great comprehensive beginner's book.

Swing trading: A guide for beginners, the best strategies for making profits in trading, forex, passive income, how to make money online in a few simple steps by Andrew J. Wolf received publication in 2019.

Join an Online Community

Another great way to learn about swing trading and meet other traders is to join an online community. There are several websites that are comprised of forums run by some of the most experienced swing traders today. These forums are extremely beneficial to any trader for a variety of reasons. First, beginners can go join the community and receive more tips, trading lessons, and other information that will help them become successful. Second, this is often a location where beginners meet their trading mentor. Third, this is a place where traders can go to not only get the most up-to-date information on the profession but also get to know people who are like them. It is always important to feel that you are not alone, especially when find yourself struggling with a part of trading. There will be hundreds, if not thousands, of people who will be interested in helping you.

Below are a few swing trading online communities that you can check out. Of course, it never hurts to check out as many communities as you can find to see which one is the best fit for you. You can do this by scanning the website to see what information is available to you, by price (unfortunately, not all the online communities are free), or by joining and figuring out over time which communities you like the most. You never know who you will meet along your journey.

The Trading Heroes Blog

This is a swing trading & currency trading education online community. This blog started in 2016 and focuses on forex education and trading. Over the last few years, this blog has grown to become one of the top swing trading blogs online. The owner publishes about one post per month; however, he is often found on the blog and is willing to help other swing traders with advice.

Elite Swing Trading

This is one of the most in-depth swing trading websites available. The site is run by Jason Bond Picks and gives not only a place where other traders can converse but also a newsletter with helpful information and tips for everyone involved in the swing trading community.

Morpheus Trading Group

This is an online community that focuses on how to trade stocks. This community started around 2002 and has steadily grown to become one of the most helpful communities online. You will receive about one post per month which will give you all types of helpful information to help you through your swing trading journey.

Ratgebergeld

If you want to find a community that gives you a little more than just one post every month, you can check out Ratgebergeld. This is a site that focuses on both swing trading and day trading. You will receive about two posts a week which focus on the most up-to-date information and a live chat. There are generally several experienced traders who are a part of this chat and are ready to help you with any problems you might be having in the moment.

Make Education a Top Priority

One of the most important factors when it comes to trading is your education. Most traders don't often take time to truly focus on their education before they start trading, which can make their journey more challenging at first. Sometimes they decide they can't afford the classes, while other times they feel that they will be able to learn better by actually performing the trades. Though both of these reasons are realistic, it is important that you do not skip the education focus. Of course, any research you complete will be part of this focus. However, there are also online classes that you can join to help you get the best handle on swing trading from the start.

Professional Swing Trading A-Z

Professional Swing Trading A-Z is one of the top trading courses which heavily discusses this topic for beginners. While you do need to pay, they will often have sale prices for their classes. Not only will you learn about the basics of swing trading but you will also get into technical analysis, fundamental analysis, various techniques and strategies, and learn how to perform a trade. On top of all this, the instructor is always available to help people who are ready or have already started their own account. Furthermore, you will learn about risk management and receive nearly 14 hours of video lessons. Unlike some courses, you don't need to have any type of previous knowledge about swing trading to take this class. In fact, you could sign up today!

Guide to Stock Trading with Candlestick and Technical Analysis

This is another course that is specifically meant for beginners who are interested in different forms of trading that focuses on stocks, such as swing trading. While you will get basic information, the majority of this class focuses on technical analysis and how to read and handle a candlestick chart. The course is run by Luca Moschini of Sharper Trade and has received high praise for being one of the best courses for the past few years. While the class is about $60, there are often sale prices that you can take advantage of.

Day Trading and Swing Trading Systems for Stocks and Options

If you have a little experience with swing trading, then you might want to check out this course. You will need some experience before you sign up for the day trading and swing trading system for stocks and options course. It is known as an intermediate course but it is very comprehensive with the topics the class covers. Udemy runs this course, in fact Udemy runs most of the courses mentioned in this section. After you pay $100 to register for the course, you will receive access to various downloadable information and hours of video lessons.

Chapter 9: Common Mistakes Beginners Make

Whether you are a beginner or expert swing trader, you will find yourself making mistakes. However, mistakes are more commonly made when you are a beginner. Before I go any further I want to let you know that this doesn't meant that you should think twice about making swing trading your new career. Mistakes are going to happen, and no one knows this better than experts. Therefore, many of them have shared their mistakes with the hope that beginners will remember the mistakes and, therefore, do what they can to avoid them.

You Have Unrealistic Expectations

There are many traders who come into the stock market world with a lot of unrealistic expectations. There are several reasons for this. For example, some might believe that trading is a career which will quickly make them rich while other people might believe that it is an easy work-from-home type job. While you can work from home when you become a swing trader, the job is not as easy as many people believe. In fact, it can be a very stressful job with a lot of factors involved from research to your post-trading analysis at the end of your work day.

In fact, when people have unrealistic expectations, it can cause a lot of problems. These problems have led many beginners to believe that they could not become a successful trader. While they didn't all quit their new career, many did. It is important to remember that you should never give up on your trading career too quickly, even if you feel that you barely know anything about trading or you realize that trading is different than what you initially thought. You should continue to research and learn about swing trading as you might like it once you get through the first few months.

The reason I am telling you that it is important to try to get through the first few months of trading is because most traders will tell you that there were many times they thought of quitting during this time. Learning trading is not an easy task. It takes a lot of dedication, patience, time, and can become very stressful at times. However, if you are truly invested in becoming a trader, you will be able to make it through these first few months. Even though you will come to realize that you had several unrealistic expectations and obstacles to go through, you were able to make it by holding on to your dedication for your new career.

If you find yourself having unrealistic expectations it is important to realize there is nothing wrong with this. In fact, you should be proud that you have noted your unrealistic expectations and can now work to change them into more realistic expectations. Furthermore, if you think about previous careers you have held, you have probably gone into your new job with unrealistic expectations. This is common when it comes to people starting new positions. One of the biggest reasons for this is because people often believe that they can take on more than they actually can when they receive a new job or even a promotion. There is always a settlement period where people start to see the reality of their new positions. During this time, they are not only learning what they can do but also what they need to work a little more on.

You Don't Follow Your Pre-Trading Analysis

I have already mentioned how important following your pre-trading analysis is. However, there are many people who start to feel that they don't need to take the time to do this for various reasons. Sometimes the reason is as simple as people are running late and just don't want to take the time when the stock market is opening. Of course, other reasons tend to follow more in the mindset that they understand how trading works and, therefore, don't need to take part in these activities anymore.

While you might feel that there is a lot of research to complete as you get your day started, you still need to make sure to take the time to check out the information. You need to make sure that you completely understand what is going on in the stock market world from the news to the changes that occurred overnight.

Of course, there have been many traders who admitted to not always following through with their pre-trading analysis. They have stated that on these days they noted they didn't perform as well. For example, they made more mistakes because they weren't briefed on the changes that the stock market made overnight or the news about a company that they held a share for. They also admitted that it made them feel like they were out of the loop in general. The stock market is constantly changing, which means you need to keep up with these changes and change with the market. If you don't take the time to do this, you will quickly fall behind.

You Don't Follow Through with Your Post-Trading Analysis

You can also quickly fall behind in the stock market world if you don't complete your post-trading analysis after the stock market closes every day. This is a very important part of your day because it will help you become a successful trader. It is important to remember that you will not become successful overnight. In fact, it takes traders years to reach the level of success that they imagine themselves reaching. This is because it takes a lot of time and practice with the stock market to not only understand it but learn all the details and tricks of the trade.

Because I discussed your post-trading analysis earlier, I am not going to spend too much more time explaining what it is. However, you should note that throughout your analysis, you need to remember to write as much down as possible. This is very important and could also be something that you change over time. For example, you might start recording the times that you made the trades during the day.

However, as you continue to analyze your post-trades over the last few months, you find out that writing down the time isn't doing anything to help you grow. In fact, you might start to see this as a worthless number. If you reach this point, you have two options. First, you can continue to write down the time because you might need this information one day. Second, you could decide to stop writing the time down. One thing to remember if you start to think about skipping the time is that you never know when you are going to need certain information in the future. While a statistic might not be helpful today, it could be helpful in a couple months.

This is one of those times where you have to remember that you are still learning all the details about swing trading. Even if you are writing down information after working as a swing trader for six months and begin to believe some of the statistics are meaningless, you should still continue to write them down. First, it is always important to remain consistent as a trader. Second, because you are learning every day, you might come across a more experienced swing trader or other information that will explain to you why this meaningless statistic is actually meaningful. When this happens, you will be grateful that you continued to write down the numbers instead of ignoring them.

You are Not Consistent

Now that I have mentioned consistency, it seems to be a good time to mention that inconsistency seems to be a common mistake that beginner traders make. Of course, there can be a variety of reasons for this from they don't remember all the steps they have to follow to they start to feel more confident in their abilities. While feeling confident is good, this shouldn't mean that you start to take your job less seriously or feel that you can skip some steps because you believe you have a better hold of what swing trading is.

You want to create a theme in your swing trading career that helps you remain consistent. Because swing trading can become a stressful career, consistency will help you maintain a healthy mental balance. Furthermore, you will be more likely to remember what you need to do and when. Of course, you will always have a trading plan or business plan to help you with these steps, it is important that you know these steps as well as you know the meaning of swing trading.

Another reason remaining consistent can help is through giving you a healthier professional and personal life balance. While some people feel that they can connect the two, more people feel that they need to create a balance in order to remain happy and content in the personal and business life. Being consistent in your job can help with this because you are more likely to follow the hours that you decide to use for your work day. For example, if you are a full-time swing trader in New York City. You might work from about 9:00 am to around 4:30 pm Monday through Friday. Even if you work at home, you want to keep these hours because this will help tell you that the hours outside of this time are reserved for your personal life.

You Don't Pay Attention to Your Mental Health

Your mental health is just as important as your physical health. However, people tend to pay less attention to their mental health. For example, when you are feeling depressed you don't often take the day off in order to get better like you would if you had a bad cold or the flu. While there are several reasons to why people tend to push their mental health aside, it is something that you need to make sure you take care of. Not only is this important for everyone, but it is important for a swing trader due to many reasons.

First, swing traders need to remain in the right mindset. Because I have discussed the right mindset previously, I am not going to go too much into that. However, I will take time to note that your mental health heavily depends on being able to reach the right mindset. For example, if you are trying to reach the right mindset, you need to be able to reach a level of confidence in yourself. If you are constantly putting yourself down for every mistake you make or you become overly critical of yourself, you will not be able to reach this right mindset. Therefore, your mental health and your right mindset to become a successful swing trader go hand in hand.

Other than making you believe that you can become a successful day trader, being mentally healthy can also help you keep from being stressed. It is important to make sure that you don't become too stressed as a trader because this can lead you into a variety of other issues from lack of confidence to making more mistakes. On top of that, becoming too stressed can cause you to make decisions based on an emotion. Stress is an emotion which often brings forth other emotions. As stated before, you want to make sure that you do not make decisions based on your emotions because you will be more likely to make a mistake or jump too quickly when you see the price of a stock fall.

Chapter 10: The 11 Commandments of Swing Trading

Some of the most experienced swing traders of 2019 like to focus on what has become known as the 11 commandments of swing trading. Popular trader, Melvin Pasternak, developed this list and discusses it after his trading classes.

1. Make Sure to Have Long Strengths and Short Weaknesses

There are two periods that you should be looking for when you are taking on a trade. The first period is known as bull and the second period is known as bear. You need to be able to identify these periods when you get into the market because this will let you know what the market conditions are like for that time.

When you look at the bull market condition, you are looking at an increasing market. The stock trends are on an upward trend, which they have been on for a good period of time. This proves that the levels of the economy are high and you should spend your time looking for longer trades.

When the market's condition is focused on bearishness, this means that the stocks are on a downward trend. The prices of stocks are dropping and many traders believe that this is the spiral that they will see in some stocks for a period of time. Bear conditions happen when the economy isn't doing very well. This is normally during points of economic recession and when unemployment is high. When you notice the bear conditions, you will want to focus on short trades as this will limit your risk of loss, especially if the downward trend continues.

2. The Overall Direction of the Market and Your Trade Should be Aligned

This is one reason research is important. You not only want to research when you are starting your swing trade profession, but you also want to continue your research. In fact, every day that you sit down in front of your desk, is a day that you will be doing research. One of these reasons is because you have to make sure to research and analyze every stock. This will help you determine whether you should purchase the stock or not.

When you are focusing on your research for a particular stock, one of the main focuses should be does the stock match the overall direction of the market? When it comes to the stock market, you will find that it's either on an upward or downward spiral. You will want to match your trade with this direction.

3. Always Look at the Long-Term Charts

One of the biggest mistakes that beginner traders often make is that they will only focus on the short-term charts when they are looking into a stock. Many experienced traders feel that this is the wrong course of action as you should have a better idea of what the trend of the stock has done over at least a six-month period. Of course, you can always go longer than six months.

You should start with the chart that will give you a couple of weeks. From there, you will want to make sure you go over the chart and notice every single detail. There is nothing that you should miss during the analysis of your chart. After you have looked at the first couple of weeks, then you can dive more into a long-term chart, such as the six-month chart. Again, follow the same microscopic process you did with the previous chart. Do your best not to miss anything. In fact, some traders will often create an excel spreadsheet where they can list everything they have to view in the chart and even write down information. This is a great piece of advice for any beginner.

4. Do Your Best Not to Enter Near the End of the Trade

Once you start to get into the stock market, you will notice a trend when it comes to traders. You will find that the stock market is busy within the first hour because there are so many traders who are buying new stocks for the day. You will then notice that the stock market begins to get quiet around the 11:00 hour because people are either holding on to their stocks or closed out for the day. However, about the last hour, which starts around 3:00 pm, you will notice the stock market picks up again as people, especially day traders, sell all their stocks and close out.

As a swing trader, you might not buy and sell stocks every day. Unlike day traders, you can hold your stocks for a few days to about a week or two. However, there are a few traders that are not allowed to do this as it would cause them too much loss.

Another reason people enter into trades earlier rather than later is because this can give you the most profit, especially if you find a stock that is hitting an upward trend. On top of this, you will have less risk to worry about if you enter a trade early. Doing your best to cut down on risk is always something traders focus on, even if they don't mind taking risks.

5. Track a Consistent Group of Stocks

Just like every trader is different, every stock is different. This is why it is important to not focus on jumping from one stock to the next. Instead, as you are learning the tricks and strategies of swing trading, you will want to start getting an idea of what kind of stocks you like. Every stock has its own personality and once you catch on to that specific personality, trading will become easier if you stick to groups of stocks that are similar.

One reason for this is because you will most likely be able to use the same strategy for all of your stocks. This can help you when it comes to learning techniques and strategies. It is easier to stick to one strategy because there are so many tiny details about swing trading you need to remember, the human brain can only hold so much information.

Another reason for this is because this allows you to be able to manage a certain amount of stocks consistently. If you are a full-time swing trader, you will find this system will give you less stress, keep your focus, and increase confidence in your abilities. Of course, all this will help you keep your right state of mind as a trader.

6. Always Have a Clear Plan

Whenever you enter a trade, you will want to make sure that you have a clear plan of action. This plan will most likely be your trading plan; however, this is known to change from time to time as traders start to learn and grow with their profession. While this is great as it means you are becoming a more successful trader, you will also want to make sure that you continue to update and adjust your plan as you need to.

Before you enter any trade, it is best to go through your plan and make sure that it will work with that stock. If you find it won't, then you will need to either adjust your trading plan or choose a stock that will fit your trading plan better.

You will want to make sure that everything is including in this plan from your entry to your exit. You will want to make sure that you have all the key points and details down. On top of this, you will also want to make sure that you have a stop-loss strategy in place so you can quickly let go of that stock through a trade and walk away from losing a large amount of money. Remember, when you decide the stop-loss strategy is the best course of action, it will happen quickly. In fact, trading is a very faced-paced business, which is another reason making sure you always have a clear plan of action is a commandment.

7. Always Integrate Fundamentals into Your Technical Analysis

While I will discuss technical analysis later in this book, one of the 11 commandments of swing trading is to make sure that you integrate fundamentals into your analysis. If you have looked into day trading, you will know a bit about fundamentals and more about technical analysis. However, when it comes to swing trading, fundamentals becomes just as important as technical analysis. The main reason for this is because you hold your stocks longer than a few minutes to a few hours.

8. Make Sure to Master the Psychological side of Swing Trading

As you will see later in this book, there is a lot of psychology that goes into swing trading. In fact, psychology goes into any type of trading, but it is more crucial when it comes to swing traders. While part of this is about keeping the right mindset, the other part comes from the overall experience of swing trading. There are a lot of factors, such as making mistakes, learning, and losing that can affect your psyche throughout your day. For example, if you take a loss you might find that you feel like a failure after you have closed out your day. This can affect your personal life as well as your working life. It is extremely important to make sure that you have a healthy frame of mind and not just the right mindset when you are a trader.

9. Try Putting the Odds in Your Favor

Sometimes you will look at a trade and wonder if you will be able to make a profit on it. This is why it is important to use technical analysis with every trade. However, even if you feel that you might not be able to make a profit, this doesn't mean that you walk away from the trade. In fact, you can take this time to work on putting the odds in your favor. While this means you might end up risking a profit, trading is always full of risks. In fact, you will never be able to fully eliminate risks. Therefore, there are times where you have to take the leap and use certain techniques in order to try to work the trade into your favor.

One way to do this is by having a target price, which should always be a part of your target plan. This price will tell you when you should quickly turn to sell or trade the stock and when you should hold on to it for a bit longer. No matter what the market conditions are, you always want to stick to your target price. Therefore, you want to make sure that you complete your technical analysis to the best of your abilities before you go forward with your trading plan.

Furthermore, it is important to not only assess the chart once but also to reassess the chart. This means that you don't just analyze the chart before you take on the trade as you will continue to look at the chart and see what the stock's trend is doing in real-time. This means that you will notice the stock price increase and decreasing throughout the time you are analyzing.

10. Trade in Harmony with the Trend Time Frames

When it comes to the stock market, there are three types of trend time frames. The longest time frame is a year. The intermediate time frame is about three months. The shortest time frame is less than a month. When you are a swing trader, you will typically focus on the intermediate and short-term time frames. However, there are traders who have stated that they have looked at trends as far back as six months. Typically, swing traders don't have to focus on the longer time frame because they are considered to be short-term traders. At the same time, swing traders need to do more than just look at the short-term trend lines.

In fact, many expert swing traders will tell beginners that if they only focus on the short-term time frame, they are more likely to make mistakes. While you can always get a good sense of what the stock is doing with the short-term time frame, this can also limit you. The stock market is a very unpredictable place. This means that the further you look back, the better your idea will be about the type of trend that goes with the stock. The key is to heavily focus on the short-term trends and then do an analysis of the intermediate trends.

11. Make Sure to Use Multiple Indicators and Not Create Isolation

Sometimes traders will often feel that they only need to use one tool to give them an idea of what stock will give them a profitable trade and what stock won't. You should never do this. You always want to make sure that you use multiple tools and that these tools give you consistent results. For example, you might use a strategy, candlestick chart, volume, and other tools in order to find out that your trade will be profitable.

One of the reasons this is important is because it helps you limit your risks. The more tools you have that give you consistent results, the more likely you are to be able to make a profit.

Chapter 11: Fundamental Analysis

When you are trying to find the best stock to take on, you want to focus on different analyses which will help you make an informed decision. One of these types of analysis is fundamental analysis. The other one is known as technical analysis, which I will cover in the next chapter. Because each of these types are extremely important, I wanted to discuss them in detail, so I decided they should have their own chapters.

Fundamental analysis is performed when you are doing general research on a company. For example, if you are interested in purchasing Amazon stock, you will start to look into the company. You might start with the company's history to get a sense of the overall growth of the entity itself. You might decide that looking over the last few years will give you enough history to help you make an informed decision. While how much research you do is more of your personal preference and how serious you take your career as a trader, I believe that the more information you have on a company, the better chance you have of becoming successful.

Fundamental Variables

There are going to be several questions that come to your mind immediately as you start to perform research on a company. For example, you might ask yourself how long the company has been successful. You might ask yourself if this is a company you believe will give you a good profit or if this company has a history of getting traders high returns. Whatever questions you ask yourself, you need to realize that you have to do more than just ask the basic questions. In fact, you have to make sure you take time to look at the fundamental variables.

Positive Earnings Adjustment

In the trading world, there are people who are known as market analysts. These are people who will often analyze how well companies are doing and then give the companies a review or a forecast, which allows other people to notice where the company is sitting. Market reviewers are typically known as cautious people and don't tend to believe that companies will pass their forecast. However, this does happen and when it does, it brings us into positive earnings adjustment.

Basically, this states that we need to look for stocks which have surprised the market analysts. This is because if companies pass their forecast, they will continue to succeed. Therefore, they become known as one of the best companies to gain a profit from, which is always a great thing for a trader to know. However, you will still want to make sure that you do your deep analysis before making any moves on a stock.

Positive Earning Revision

This is the process that market analysts go through when they are evaluating how well a company is doing so they can give them a forecast. As stated above, these analysts are cautious and very careful to note where they think the company is going. Therefore, when the company goes farther than what they initially thought, they need to re-evaluate the company. Of course, admitting they are wrong is not an easy thing for analysts to do as it isn't easy for anyone. However, when they do need to admit this, people can quickly learn what companies they should start paying attention to.

Earnings Momentum

While there are many important fundamental variables to look at when you are making an analysis, earnings momentum holds a special place. This variable is very important, especially when it comes to bull markets. Earnings momentum is the variable which looks at the year to year growth of earnings. Therefore, this is what will often set the price for stocks.

Strong Cash Flow

This is another fundamental variable that will tell you how much free cash a company has. This is a very important variable because it will let you know where a company financially sits after it has paid all of its bills and expenses. When you are getting into trading, you want to pay attention to the companies who are financially stable. You want to make sure that a company can grow because the more they grow, the more profit that you can make. Think about it – if you put your money into a stock where the company could barely pay the electric bill, do you think that your money would be secure, if even for a period of time? You want to make place your money in companies which are financially secure.

Earnings Growth

Another variable you want to pay attention to is how much more money the company is making as the years go on. When you look at this variable, you will be looking at the earnings growth variable. This is another company that you would think of investing in because you know that they have seen considerable growth for a certain number of years. Therefore, you analyze that the company will only continue to grow.

Chapter 12: Technical Analysis

Technical analysis is as important as fundamental analysis, especially when it comes to swing trading. However, you could view technical analysis as the more serious of the two types of analysis. Instead of just looking at the basics of the company and the fundamental variables which focus on your potential stock's company, you will focus more on the technical side of your stock when you look at technical analysis.

By definition, technical analysis is measuring the historical trends of the stock. Because many people feel that technical analysis is trickier than fundamental analysis, it might be wise to do more research about the topic before you start analyzing any stocks. There are a few online classes and books that are available for you, if you feel the need to become well educated on technical analysis.

One of the biggest factors to remember when you are focusing on technical analysis is you want to make sure to study every detail of your stock's history. You want to make sure you understand the trend, have made any notes you needed to, and that you believe you see the trend giving you the best profit before you decide to take on the stock. Technical analysis is going to take time and patience. However, you also don't want to spend too much time trying to decide if you want to take on a specific stock or not. This is a special time balance that you will figure out once have opened your account and on your way to trading stocks.

What You Will Study Through Technical Analysis

There are several details of the stock's history that you will look at when you are focusing on the technical analysis part of your trading schedule. This is something that you will do with every stock as it will help you decide if this stock is going to be worth your energy and time.

In order to give you a better view of what type of things you will look for, I will briefly discuss them below.

Study of Charts

Of course, one of the main pieces of the stock you will look at are the historical charts. These charts will give you some of the most detailed information that will help you make the best decision possible for your swing trading journey.

One of the most common charts are known as candlestick charts. These charts received this name because they are shaped like a candlestick. On top of that, the information you will find in the chart is designed through the candlestick. There are two main reasons why traders like candlestick charts so much. First, these charts are fairly easy to read and understand. Not only do they give you the information you need to know but they will also show off colors. The second reason is because these charts are known to give you an indication that the trend is about to change. For many people, this is extremely helpful because it decreases the amount of research that you need to do. However, there are other people that still say you should always perform your own research to make sure that the candlestick chart is correct on its assumption.

In general, the candlestick chart will tell you what the opening price was for the stock, the highest price, the lowest price, and the closing price. By getting these prices, you will start to analyze the chart to see what type of trend this stock is following. By looking at the history of the stock, you can start to get a sense of what the average prices are throughout the day. On top of this, you will also be able to get a sense of how much the stock tends to jump up and down during the day. On top of this, the candlestick chart will change colors in the center, depending on if the stock made a profit that day between the opening and closing price. For example, if the candlestick color is white or green, then you will know that the opening price was lower than the closing price. If you see a red or black color, then you will know that the opening price was higher than the closing price.

Of course, you will want to do this type of analysis for any chart that you come across, whether it is a line or pie chart. While each chart will look a bit different, they will all have the same valuable information within them. They will all tell you what the prices were throughout the day. However, not all of the charts will give you a prediction to what the trend will be doing next.

Volume

Another major part of technical analysis is the volume of a stock. The reasons why the volume is so important is because you will be able to get a sense of the intensity of the stock's movement in price. What this means is you will be able to take a certain amount of time, whether it is a few hours or a few months and get an idea of how many shares were traded during this time. Of course, the more shares that you find are traded, the better the stock is for trading. Stocks tend to reach high volume for many reasons. For example, they could be considered one of the more popular trading stocks on the market, such as Apple or Target. Another reason is because higher volume tends to mean a better profit. Think about it – people don't often take on trades where they are less likely to make a profit. Therefore, if the volume is high you know that most traders have found this stock to be successful.

Analyzing the Trend Line

I have already discussed a lot of information about trend lines in this book. By now, you should know that it is one of the main factors that will help you determine the success rate of a stock and whether you want to take on this stock or not. However, I feel it is important to mention that whenever you are analyzing a trend line, you are using technical analysis. You are not only analyzing what the trend line has done the previous day or the last couple of days, but you are most likely looking at the trend line over a period of months. The farther back you go, the more you will be able to learn details about the stock's trends.

Chapter 13: Managing Risk

One of the most important factors of any type of trading is learning how to manage risk. Of course, this is also one of the trickiest areas in this profession. While there are a lot of techniques and tips that can help you manage risk, you will never be able to completely eliminate risk. In fact, there is always some type of risk, no matter what stock you take on. You can decide to buy Amazon or Netflix, which are two of the best swing trading stocks on the market for 2019 and find yourself losing capital instead of gaining money. If this happens, it is simply because you didn't do everything you could at first to make sure that your risk was at a manageable level.

On top of this, you might have used the wrong strategy for the stock or not read the chart correctly. Remember, the prices of stocks are going up and down throughout the day. Furthermore, a downward spiral can find itself lower than the opening price of that day. Therefore, you always want to do what you can to make sure that you sell your stock at the correct time. If you find yourself losing money and realize you will probably be unable to make a profit, you will want to use your stop-loss strategy in order to get out of the trade as soon as possible as this will limit your loss.

How to Limit Your Risk

When it comes to trading in the stock market, it really doesn't matter what type of trading you are a part of, the ways to limit risk are generally the same. Most of them are pretty basic, and some have already been covered when I discussed some of the most common mistakes or tips for beginners. However, there are several that I didn't touch on, so I could give you some of the best ways to focus on limiting your risk in this chapter.

Keep Your Emotions in Check

While I have briefly touched on this before, I want to talk about making sure you can keep your emotions in check while trading in more detail. It is a very important factor to remember and once that can decrease your risk greatly.

One of the best examples to give you when it comes to the importance of keeping your emotions in check is the stock market crash of 1929. One of the reasons this crash occurred was because investors and traders started to let their emotions take over as they saw the stock market numbers decrease. How the numbers work is this way – when people are buying the stock, the price of the stock will increase. This also means that your profit is going up. However, when the price of the stock decreases, this means that people are selling. Furthermore, it means that you are losing money. Therefore, when the people on the New York Stock Exchange in October saw the prices of stock dropping at a fast rate, most decided to quickly sell their stocks because they wanted to make sure they received as much profit as possible. On top of this, people were starting to fear what was going to happen to the stock market. Because of their emotions, they started to make irrational decisions about selling their stocks. Therefore, part of the reason for the stock market crash was because investors and traders let their emotions take over instead of focusing on thinking rationally.

The basis of controlling your emotions when it comes to making decisions in the stock market is to make sure you are making the most logical decision that you can. There is a lot of critical thinking that goes into deciding if you want to purchase or sell a stock. Many people can begin to feel overwhelmed, which can lead to a variety of negative emotions such as stress. When this happens, you are less likely to be able to think clearly, which is an important piece of critical thinking and keeping your emotions in check.

Furthermore, people can become greedy when they begin to see they are making a profit as a trader. Like with any other job, the more money people are making, the more money they want to receive. This is often a human reaction when it comes to money but it can also lead to people becoming greedy if this reaction is not kept in check. When traders become greedy, they start to look for the stocks that they believe will make the most money. When this happens, they are more likely to miss certain details about the stock, including the overall trend of the stock.

While trading is a stressful and exciting career, which are both strong emotions people feel, it is also a career that should not mix with your emotions. The less your emotions show as a trader, the more likely you will be to make sure you make the right decisions.

Keeping your emotions in check is especially important when you find a stock going against you. Not only does this make you realize that you made a mistake during your analysis and any calculations, which carries its own emotions, but this can also make you go through a series of emotional stages. There are many traders and investors who state that this series of five stages is similar to the five stages of grief. While some people feel that this is a bit over-dramatic, several experienced traders have discussed how they often feel these stages when they see a big loss from one of their stocks.

The five stages include:

1. Denial

When a trader reaches the stage of denial, they feel that they can't believe that the stock turned on them because it seemed like such as great move. Sometimes it takes the trader a while to realize that they are in a bad situation and about to lose a lot of money.

2. Anger

This is the stage where traders start to not only get mad at the stock market and other traders but also at themselves. While some will start to think that the stock market is against them, or blame the short sellers for their situations, other traders will become overly critical of themselves. During this time, they might become angry at themselves for not following their trading plan or for making a mistake.

3. Bargaining

The bargaining stage can occur before or right after they actually lose the money. While they have moved passed the first two stages, they still feel that there is something they can do. This is when some traders start trying to find a way out of the situation, such as asking God or another higher power to let them break even so they don't lose a huge amount of money.

4. Depression

At this point, traders will start to go over their plan and start to question what they did wrong. They start to feel depressed because they now realize that they have officially lost the money and there is no way to get the money back. They might start to dwell during this process and continue to become overly critical of themselves. However, instead of being angry, they might wonder why they didn't pay enough attention to their trading plan or the steps they were taking.

It is important to realize during this step that, unless a trader find himself in bad debt, he is most likely not in any type of clinical depression. While it is called depression, it is more like a sadness that can last anywhere from a couple of hours to a couple of days. However, if you do find yourself more in a depression because you ended up losing all of the money in your account and possibly still owe your broker, you might want to think of looking at counseling help. This is nothing to be ashamed about. In fact, there have been several traders who have found themselves in a depression because they sent themselves and their families into debt. As stated many times, trading can be a risky business and even some of the most experienced traders can make bad decisions that can cost them a lot of money.

5. Acceptance

This is the final step in the grief cycle. It is the step where while you might still be feeling a bit sad or a sense of guilt over losing so much money, but you accept that the situation has happened and close out your trade. You then do what you can to deal with the situation and continue on with your career. At this point, it is important to remember that just because you lost a lot of money doesn't mean you should end your trading career. As stated before, mistakes happen in the stock market. The best option you can do once you find yourself losing money is close out so you don't lose more money than you have to, learn from your mistake, and move on.

Follow the 1% Rule

One of the biggest ways to reduce your risk is to make sure that you focus on keeping your proportion low. One of the best ways to do this is to only risk about 1% of the money in your account with each trade. For example, if you have $10,000 in your account, this means that you will not trade more than $100 on a trade. However, many expert swing traders believe that when you are first starting out, you should lower this even more. Therefore, a beginner should look at trading no more than around 0.3% to 0.5%. While this doesn't seem like a lot of money, most stocks generally aren't a large amount of money to buy. Some of the most expensive stocks to buy will be blue-chip stocks.

Of course, there are always traders who often thrive on risk, which means that following the 1% rule won't feel comfortable to them. While this isn't advised for beginners, if you find yourself more comfortable taking higher risks, then you should think about increasing the percentage. For instance, instead of 1%, you could go up to 2% or 3%. However, it is not recommended that you go much higher than that. It really all depends on your personal preference with risk, your experience, and how much capital you have in your account.

One thing to think about before you decide on your percentage is how much capital you can lose if you find yourself in a losing streak. Think of it this way – if you have $25,000 in your account (which is often minimum) and you find yourself putting 2% of your capital into a couple of different trades that you lose on both, you are going to find yourself losing a lot of money quickly. While you can always add more money into your account every time, you can easily see how this can affect your finances.

On top of that, losing can affect a person psychologically, especially when you are losing money. People generally take losing money more seriously than losing a lot of other things. Part of this is because we are so dependent on money. We need money to pay for our home, our vehicles, groceries, and other bills. Furthermore, we need money to purchase the things we want, including stocks. Therefore, when you find your amount of capital decreasing rapidly in your account, you're going to start feeling affected psychologically, which is going to affect you emotionally. Of course, this can cause a whole new set of problems when it comes to trading, as we have already discussed.

Determine a Stop-Loss Amount

However, just how can you determine the right proportion size for your account? There are actually factors that can help you with this. After you have looked at setting your risk at 1%, you can look at another factor, which is setting your trade risk. This is when you set your stop-loss amount. This amount will be created when you set up your trading plan. For example, if you spent $10.00 on your trade, then you might set up your stop-loss level at $9.80. This means that once you reach this amount, you will sell that stock and only lose .20 cents. Most traders will look at the percentage of their account they put towards their stock in order to help them determine their stop-loss amount. This is because some traders might feel more comfortable setting their stop-loss amount at a higher percentage if they followed the 1% rule than a if they decided to go up to 3% or even 5%.

Follow Your Guidelines and Rules

We have already discussed various way to help you eliminate risk when we discussed some of the common mistakes and various tips for beginners. These are important to follow as they will help you eliminate risk. For example, making sure you stay in the right mindset will help you remain positive about trading. This can help you eliminate your risk because you will continue to put your best effort into making sure that you make the best decisions when it comes to your trades.

As you get started in your trading career, you will start to develop your own rules and guidelines, such as in your trading plan. It is important that you don't change any of these rules and guidelines without fully looking at your trade as a whole. On top of this, it is important to follow because it will help keep you focused, you will begin to learn the details of swing trading easier as you won't be so concerned about your next step, and you will feel more comfortable in your abilities.

Don't Trade Alone

Earlier I discussed the importance of finding a broker as they will not only help you with your trades, but they will also advise you through your swing trading career. This is especially important for beginners as it is a great way to lower your risk. There is a lot you will still learn as you start to trade. Even when you begin trading with simulations, which means you don't use real money, to get a feel of what trading in the stock market is really like; you will still feel different once you start using real money. Therefore, it is important to make sure that you have someone you trust that you can bring your questions, concerns, and can help teach you how to manage your account and all the other facts that go into trading.

Of course, this doesn't mean that you always need a broker. In fact, there are a lot of swing traders who don't have brokers. However, at first, you should always make sure that you have someone to help guide you until you learn the world of swing trading a little better and become more comfortable making decisions on your own. For example, you might have a broker for the first couple of years you are a swing trader and then decide that you are content with making your own decisions.

It's important to note that just because swing traders don't have a broker doesn't mean they don't get advice or information from other traders to help them along in their career. Every swing trader will tell you that no matter where you are in your career or how comfortable you are with trading, you should always be a part of an online forum. Even if you decide to create your own swing trading forum one day, you will still continue to communicate with people who will help you along your swing trading journey. This is important as the people you find in your online communities will start to become similar to your co-workers. Having people who have similar interests and understand the factors that go into the job, such as the risk, stress, level of commitment, and excitement will help you remain successful in your career. They will help you stick to the right mindset.

Chapter 14: The Psychology of Swing Trading

Many traders would never imagine that there is psychology in the world of swing trading. However, if you think about it, there is a lot of psychology in trading. In fact, you wouldn't be able to trade or become a successful trader if you didn't include psychology in the field. Not only do you use psychology when you are analyzing your research and information, but you also use psychology when you are focusing on your winning mindset and making sure you are mentally healthy.

In general, psychology is the study of the mind. While this might seem like a strange thing to include when trading, if you think about it, you are always critically thinking when you are working as a trader. You are always thinking about the charts you are seeing, you are always observing what is going on around you, so you can make note on the conditions of the stock market and your environment for your trading journal. On top of this, you are analyzing yourself as a trader, so you can become the best swing trader possible. All of this requires using the mind to analyze, which is basically studying the mind. However, instead of studying someone else's mind as psychologists usually do, you are studying your own mind.

One of the biggest ways psychology becomes a part of swing trading is by teaching you to analyze the reports and charts you see on a daily basis. Through analyzing the ways in which the stock market prices go up and down, the closing price, and the opening price you are able to piece together an average price. On top of this, as you continue to analyze the charts by going back in history to look at previous days and then analyze the general conditions of the stock market, you will be able to start to note what direction the stock is going to take. You will start to see a pattern and you will be able to think about where the pattern is going to go next to see if you should invest in this stock or not.

Another huge way psychology is a part of trading is through your trading journal. Whether you use charts and make notes, write in a journal, or both you will be writing down various pieces of information that will help you look at yourself as a trader. Through this, you will be able to see what your strengths are, what your weaknesses are, where you tend to feel the most stress, and what you still need to research when it comes to the stock market. Without being able to analyze yourself, you wouldn't be able to figure out all this information to help you become a successful trader.

Finally, psychology has a lot to do with your mental health. While I have discussed this, it is important to take time to explain how this ties into psychology. The easiest way to think about this is by realizing that your peace of mind, which is your ability to remain calm so you don't become stressed and then allow other emotions to creep up and influence your decision-making is tied to trading results. In fact, these factors are all tied to your trading results.

When you are doing well – you are not only making a good amount of profit, but you are limiting your mistakes and are completing your daily tasks, you begin to feel confident in your abilities. When this happens, you start to feel happier, you start to feel more relaxed, and you start to become more determined. In fact, many experienced traders have stated that the more confident you are in your abilities as a trader, the more determined you will be. This will help you because you will start to focus more on your responsibilities and begin to perform better overall.

When you are doing poorly – you are seeing more capital loss than capital gains, you are making more mistakes, and you are having trouble completing your daily tasks, you begin to feel poorly. Not only does your mental health start to decline, but you will stop paying attention to what you eat. You won't get enough sleep and, overall, you will stop taking care of yourself as well as you do when you are mentally healthy. All these factors will affect your trading results. You won't perform as well as you did when your mental health was stronger.

Because most people don't think of this, it is important to note. You need to realize that your energy level, alertness, confidence, and overall health (mental, emotional, and physical) will affect your trading results. Because of this, in order to become the best trader that you can be, you want to make sure you are doing everything you can in order to increase your mental health. The best benefit of doing this is that you will not only find yourself handling your swing trading career better, but you will also feel better in your personal life. In fact, making sure you are in an overall healthy state will help you in all areas of your life.

At this point, it is important to note that no matter how you mentally feel, everyone has some improvement to work on mentally. If you begin to realize that you are overly critical of yourself, you lack confidence, or you struggle in other ways, you are not alone. You can further work to improve your mental health in a variety of ways so you can become a successful swing trader.

Maintain Your Mental Health

There are dozens of ways to help you maintain your mental health. I won't be able to cover them all in this book, but I will focus on several to give yourself different techniques to choose from so you can help build up your mental health.

Make Sure You Get Enough Sleep

Many people do not understand how not getting enough sleep can affect your mental health. In fact, in can affect it in more than one way. First, when you don't get enough sleep, you are just not as alert as you should be. When this happens, your mental health is affected because it doesn't feed off your positive emotions as it should. It's not that being less alert makes you depressed, it is simply that your body is trying to conserve energy, therefore, your mind doesn't receive the energy it needs to keep your mental state healthy.

Another way not getting enough sleep can affect your mental health is by giving up on tasks easier. Because you are tired and sluggish, you don't have the energy to deal with your regular daily tasks. This can have a downfall on your mental health. Instead of feeling like you are accomplishing your tasks, you begin to feel like you are wasting your time and that you won't be able to complete your tasks successfully. Of course, this can make you feel less confident in your abilities. While feeling like this rarely won't affect your mental health much in the long term, it can in the short term. On top of this, if you get in the habit of not getting enough sleep, you will find your mental health decreasing rapidly.

Focus on the Positive

One of the biggest ways to boost your mental health is to focus on the positive. While there are many negative things that are going to happen to you on a daily basis, it is important to make sure that you focus on the positive things that happen. For example, if you accomplish a task, take a moment to reflect on this task and be proud of your accomplishment. This will not only help boost your self-esteem, but it will also help you get rid of any negativity you were feeling.

Practice Self-Control

Self-control is an important factor when it comes to trading and mental health. When it comes to trading, you want to make sure you are practicing self-control because you will become more likely to accomplish the tasks you need to, stick to your schedule, and follow any techniques, strategies, and tips that you are given so you can become a successful trader.

When it comes to mental health, it is important to practice self-control because you will be better able to control your thoughts. You can train your mind, in a sense, to focus more on the positive. For example, many psychologists will give their clients who focus on the negative a task. This task simply states that for any negative thought they have they need to replace it with two positive thoughts. While this can become more of a challenge for people at first, the more the practice it, the more they will gain self-control over their thoughts. They will start realizing when they are thinking negatively and immediately start focusing on positive thoughts. Because positivity is more likely to give you better trading results, this will help improve yourself as a swing trader.

Conclusion

Congratulations for making it to the end of this book! I know it was a lot of information for you to take in, so this is really an accomplishment in your swing trading career!

One of the goals of this book was to give you a start on your swing trading career. Not only did I want to explain the key concepts of financial trading. Because this is considered to be a foundation when it comes to trading, I didn't want to leave this information out of the book. On top of this, it was important to explain to you the difference between trading and investing. There are a lot of people who get into trading when they believed they were going to be investing money instead of trading stocks in order to gain a profit. Because these two topics are different, it is important to make sure you want to be a trader and not an investor before you go too far into your research for swing trading.

Another major point of this book was to give you a concise beginner's guide about swing trading which touched on a variety of topics. Instead of you having to read dozens more articles and a few books about swing trading, I wanted to give you a way that you can place one book in your device to turn to when you need a refresher about swing trading. On top of this, I wanted you to be able to bring this book to your friends who are interested in swing trading and show them this beginner's guide, so they can get all the information required before opening their account with a broker.

As you have realized by this point, swing trading is not the easiest career; however, when it comes to the stock market, there is no easy career. It doesn't matter if you decide on swing trading, become a buy and hold investor, or get into day trading you will find that each one of these areas have their own challenges. However, you will soon come to find that they each have their own advantages as well. You should already to be able to pick out a few advantages to becoming a swing trader. For example, you could one day be able to trade without the assistance of a broker. On top of this, you have been able to get a sneak peak of the many online communities for swing traders. Once you decide to join an online community or two, you will realize how enjoyable swing trading is.

You should also understand what simulation trading is and how important it is to make sure you complete this type of trading before you start trading for money. You should also not only understand risks which are associated in swing trading but also have an idea on how to decrease these risks once you start swing trading. Of course, this is one reason you want to make sure to practice simulation trading at first. As stated before, simulation trading will help you make sure that you understand the risks and the strategies which are associated with swing trading.

By now you should not only clearly understand what swing trading is, but also what the average time fame is for a swing trader. You should be able to remember the 11 commandments of swing trading, techniques, what the right mindset is when you are trading, know a variety of tips to help you get on your way, and also understand the many mistakes that other swing traders have made.

Furthermore, you should be able to explain how a day will go for a full-time swing trader, be able to explain the two different types of stock market conditions, and the art of short selling.

On top of all the information you need to know about being a swing trader, you also know how to get started with researching as much information as possible. On top of this, you have learned tips to help you become a better researcher, so you can gain the most out of your research time. It is important to keep these tips in mind as you will need to used them throughout your career. On top of this, you can also add your own tips, which will become useful when you begin to help other beginner swing traders in the next few years.

Thank you for not only purchasing this book but also reading it. I hope that you found it helpful in your swing trading journey. I wish you the best of luck!

Bibliography

Chen, J. (2019). Short Selling is Risky But Rewarding. Retrieved from https://www.investopedia.com/terms/s/shortselling.asp.

Chen, J. (2019). Exploring How Exchange-Traded Fund – ETFs Work. Retrieved from https://www.investopedia.com/terms/e/etf.asp.

Five Problems Often Caused By Unrealistic Trading Expectations. (2018). Retrieved from https://vantagepointtrading.com/setting-realistic-expectations-forex-trader/

Folger, J. (2019). Investing vs. Trading: What's the Difference?. Retrieved from https://www.investopedia.com/ask/answers/12/difference-investing-trading.asp

Folger, J. (2017). How to Start Trading. Retrieved from https://www.investopedia.com/university/how-start-trading/

Fuller, N. (2018). How To Develop A Winning Trader's Mindset » Learn To Trade The Market. Retrieved from https://www.learntotradethemarket.com/forex-articles/how-to-develop-a-winning-traders-mindset.

Gerry, L. (2013). 10 Signs You're Burning Out -- And What To Do About It. Retrieved from https://www.forbes.com/sites/learnvest/2013/04/01/10-signs-youre-burning-out-and-what-to-do-about-it/#fbfde2b625b4

Gray, S. (2019). Swing Trading: A Comprehensive Beginner's Guide to Learning Swing Trading from A-Z. Kindle Edition.

Hall, M. (2019). Introduction to Swing Trading. Retrieved from https://www.investopedia.com/trading/introduction-to-swing-trading/

How to Choose the Best Online Broker for Trading Stocks. Retrieved from https://www.swing-trade-stocks.com/online-brokers.html

Lowe, M. (2019). Swing Trading: A Beginner's Guide to Highly Profitable Swing Trades - Proven Strategies, Trading Tools, Rules, and Money Management. Kindle Edition.

Mitchell, C. (2018). The Easiest Way to Keep

a Trading Journal — a Great Tool. Retrieved from https://www.thebalance.com/how-to-keep-a-trading-journal-the-easy-way-and-why-1031236.

Pezim, B. (2018). How To Swing Trade: A Beginner's Guide to Trading Tools, Money Management, Rules, Routines and Strategies of a Swing Trader. Kindle Edition.

Swing Trading Basics | Learn the Basics of Swing Trading. Retrieved from https://www.swing-trade-stocks.com/swing-trading-basics.html

The Stop-Loss Order — Make Sure You Use It. (2019). Retrieved from https://www.investopedia.com/articles/stocks/09/use-stop-loss.asp.

Vonko, D. (2017). Fundamental Analysis for Traders. Retrieved from https://www.investopedia.com/articles/trading/06/fundamentalapproach.asp.

What is financial trading?. Retrieved from https://www.ig.com/en/learn-to-trade/what-is-financial-trading.

www.ingramcontent.com/pod-product-compliance
Lightning Source LLC
Chambersburg PA
CBHW030519210326
41597CB00013B/960